ANNE HOOPER

28 DAYS TO
FABULOUS
SEX

A complete sex-life makeover

DK

London, New York, Munich, Melbourne, Delhi

Brand Manager for Anne Hooper Lynne Brown
Senior editor Peter Jones
Project art editor Claire Legemah
Senior art editor Helen Spencer
US editor Margaret Parrish
DTP designers Karen Constanti, Jackie Plant, Traci Salter
Production controller Shwe Zin Win
Photography Russell Sadur
Jacket designer Chloe Alexander
Jacket editor Carrie Love
Publishing director Corinne Roberts
Art director Carole Ash

First American Edition 2005

00 01 02 03 04 05 06 07 08 10 9 8 7 6 5 4 3 2 1

First published in the United States in 2005 by
DK Publishing, Inc.
375 Hudson Street,
New York, New York 10014

A Cataloging-in-Publication record for this book is available
from the Library of Congress.

ISBN 0-7566-0524-5

Reproduced in Singapore by Colourscan
Printed in Singapore by Star Standard

See our complete product line at
www.dk.com

contents

introduction

BEING UNFIT AND HEAVY doesn't necessarily mean that your sexual response will be altered. But it certainly does mean that your sexual performance is. And for all those who have fought the food battles and more or less survived, there are many others who have lost the fight. One in three individuals in the US is now not just overweight, but obese. And that's not counting the majority who are not actually obese but are somewhere on the road to Fatsville.

So this book is about sexual fitness and unashamedly focuses on streamlining the body. It is not intended for teenagers (unless grossly overweight) since young people should wait until they have reached their full adult shape before even thinking about dieting. But it is aimed at anyone over 21 who wants to make the most of their health and sexual versatility and remain youthful. And yes, you can still be youthful in middle age if you pay attention to your body and listen to what it's telling you.

four ways to fabulous sex

This book focuses on four specific points of action.

Eating Find out what suits your particular digestion so that food feels comfortable inside you. If you've ever tried making love while suffering from indigestion after food that did not suit you, you will understand what I mean.

Patterning Teach your brain to learn new eating patterns so that it doesn't automatically fall back on the old, unhealthy ones.

Body strengthening Perform simple exercises, both physical and sexual, so that your muscles are accustomed to movement and carry out your commands with ease.

Sexual choice Discover when your body feels right for sex and pay attention when it says no. Too many people expect their body to operate like clockwork, always to be ready for sexual expression when, in fact, this is never automatically the case.

We need to rediscover how to listen to our bodies, and being aware of our digestive process is the key to doing so.

You can streamline your body shape, lose weight, and then maintain a healthy eating pattern. There have always been exercises that benefit sexual expression and performance, but we need to lose some of our defensiveness about doing them. Be bold, and acknowledge that part of the reason for keeping in shape is to be healthy and sexy. And, although I never believe you should adopt certain sex positions because somebody says you should, I know that lots of people want ideas because it gives them a choice. So all the sexual exercises and positions described here are optional—there for you if you want them; not required if you don't.

I am the first to know how hard it is to stick to a healthy eating pattern. As a chocoholic I'm aware how all first principles fly out of the window when you notice a new chocolate bar on the market, which of course you simply have to sample. The remedy that has really worked for me is that if you learn to eat your food in a very clear-cut pattern, that pattern eventually enters your subconscious and starts operating automatically. After all, it's what happens without our knowing it when we learn to eat in the first place as children.

A combination of this eating pattern plus Pilates training has slimmed and strengthened me. It means that I have sufficient strength to play a proactive role in lovemaking and enough body flexibility to have fun with some of the sillier sex positions. And the whole combination of good health and an easy sexuality means I do feel good. I feel happy. It would be wonderful if you could feel the same too. That's what this book is about!

Let me know how your 28-Day Plan goes.

Anne J. Hooper

how the book works

Chapter one helps you diagnose how sexually fit you are, plus how to decide what you want from sex.

Chapter two describes the physical training you can use if you want to hone the very specific muscles used during energetic sexual activity. This section is purely optional. If you hate the idea, leave it out.

Chapter three focuses on what specific foods do for you plus it comes up with some great ideas for foodie sex.

Chapter four consists of the 28-Day Plan, which allows you to train your eating habits to follow a healthy pattern while opting for a good diet in the first place. It also suggests sexual activity to suit the changes that your digestive system will be undergoing. This is so that sex feels wonderful and rewarding instead of a painful strain. This section also gives you some bright ideas on how to adapt the plan and make it fun for you.

your sex life

GOOD SEX is about the loving mingling of mind and body, where each aspect of being interacts to provide a wonderful emotional and physical experience. Most sex manuals focus on the technical and therapeutic sides to sex, few on the health and fitness aspects of lovemaking. Yet, we are living in a time of unprecedented food supply in the Western world, where previously unheard of numbers of people are clinically obese. What can such obesity be doing to their sex lives? In this first section you are helped to evaluate how physically fit for sex you may be.

a lot of sex is good for you

Why a sexual diet book? Why not just a diet and exercise book? Sex is a great incentive to getting fit and gives meaning to lives, a reason for physical self-improvement, and powerful health benefits and advantages.

THERE IS NO DOUBT that the experience of regular, good sex is nurturing. Men and women who love each other interpret sexual intercourse as caring or being cared for. The experience of touch alone is soothing, while sexual intercourse allows the greatest expanse of your body to get as close to the greatest expanse of another as physically possible. People, who are lovingly, confidently touched, feel confident themselves, are able to tackle the world, and are happy. Touch works at every age and every aspect of life. Touch soothes babies, helps heal patients, socializes delinquents, and is the pathway for developing loving intimacy. Sex is the ultimate experience of touch and, at its best, leads to comfort of the body and (very occasionally) ecstasy of the mind.

what a man can give to a woman

The mingling of sexual love juices can mean actual health benefits for men and women. A woman receives minute portions of testosterone as a result of her lover's orgasm, (provided of course that she doesn't use barrier methods of contraception). On a regular basis, this chemical might contribute toward her energy levels, sexual sensitivity, healthy libido, and physical fitness. Clinical observation shows that women who continue regular intercourse with their partner into and during old age retain better shape and condition in their vaginal organs, with more lubrication and greater flexibility, than those who do not. Women naturally lose testosterone from the body during menopause and after, but those who are encouraged to remain sexually active often do not need as much extra vaginal lubrication or testosterone replacement. The interior of the vagina consists of moist mucous membrane, which absorbs substances (such as testosterone) as easily as the moist membrane of the mouth and tongue.

what a woman can give to a man

There is recent evidence to show that orgasm decreases the risk of prostate problems in men. Men don't necessarily need a loving partner in order to ejaculate but a sizeable majority who continue to enjoy sex into old age gain other benefits. Take the artist Picasso, who was almost as famous for his incredibly long and active sex life as he was for his painting. Statistics show that as many as three-quarters of men stop having sexual intercourse by the time they reach the age of 75. Picasso was not only still having sex (and fathering children), but most of important, was still alive. This is not as silly a statement as it sounds. Some 80 percent of men are likely to contract prostate difficulties later if not sooner, and prostate cancer kills. If sexual intercourse can stave it off, it makes sense to get as sexually fit as you possibly can!

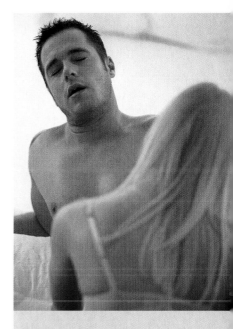

extra health advantages

• The experience of orgasm may prevent aggressive feelings and lead to calmer management of everyday problems.

• Sex boosts the immune system: it has also been found to counter breast cancer development.

• Orgasm releases endorphins: these are feel-good chemicals that act as both relaxant and painkiller.

• Women who experience regular sex also experience increased estrogen levels; these improve the condition of skin and hair, and redress menopausal hormone imbalances.

• Sex allows couples to take mildly aerobic exercise without really being aware of it. Sexual intercourse benefits lungs, heart, and muscle groups.

what do you really want?

Although fitness does not guarantee good sex, a streamlined body does assist the inner self, provided that exercise is not taken to extremes so that the body becomes unbalanced.

EXPERIMENTS HAVE SHOWN THAT improvements in appearance and fitness go hand in hand with the attainment of sexual confidence. Inner confidence is, after all, the happiness and relaxation of your inner persona—the inner man or woman.

the inner you

It doesn't matter which attribute of health or sexuality you tackle first. Each has its effect on the other. One person may want to start improving their sexual health with new sex positions, another with physical exercise, a third with boosting libido, and a fourth with inner digestion. This book explains

all four sexual fitness options. The choice, of which aspect to start with, is left totally up to you, the reader.

Don't agonize about your decision. The overall mantra of this book is to cut down anxiety levels and enjoy what you have got. And the important message of the book is that YOU—the inner you—is fine and worth loving. Just about anything can be changed with regards to the outer you and those changes may help you feel good about yourself. But in the long run, it's the inner you that really matters.

improving the sexual fit

For example, with some partners sex may not work very well. This does not mean you are a failure. What it probably means is that you and this person are a poor fit sexually. But… and it's a big but… you can learn how to have sex together; you can learn how to communicate verbally; you can let the tips of your finger and the touch of your skin talk. You can even learn how to communicate in bed—something incredibly difficult for many of us. In other words it is honestly possible to become sexually fit, something that allows you good choices during lovemaking. Take a look at some of the fitness options on the right, then turn over to assess your fitness options.

how to be strong and sexy

Here are your starting points to fitness and overall health:
• Assess your strengths and weaknesses. In other words, know yourself.
• Hone your physical flexibility and core body strength, especially core pelvic strength.
• Adopt a healthy Mediterranean diet that allows your body to adjust slowly in size and health. With modifications such a diet can be adjusted to help fight obesity or to strengthen and build your body if you have been too thin.
• Lose health-sapping addictions such as too much alcohol, tobacco, or drugs.
• Exercise with specific sexual positions in mind.
• Mentally examine yourself regularly to make sure you are not OD-ing on diet or exercise. Overdoing any regimen can create personal tensions that block sexual sensation.
• Take seriously the quality of the food you put into your body and the physical effect it exerts on your digestive tolerance. If you feel sluggish, you will end up sluggish in your lovemaking.
• Be aware of the journey that food takes through your body. Is your body facilitating that journey? Is your digestive system aiding your freshness and fitness?

how sexy do you feel?

WE ALWAYS WANT TO KNOW more about sex. Do friends and neighbors share in the incredible sensations we have managed to experience? How do we compare with them? Are there ways in which we might please a partner more? Is it possible that we might become better lovers than we already are? These are just some of the questions we might ask ourselves.

A not-so-good day might also raise the following: Am I attractive? Am I any good as a lover? Could I enjoy the experience of sex more? Could my partner enjoy the experience of sex more? And so on. So how do you go about discovering your sexual potential? How do you find out if you and your lover could get even sexier?

the sex tests

The following series of questions and physical exercises, spread out over the next few pages, is intended to give you enough information about your sexuality to answer some of the above questions. The information you learn will offer you a platform for changing and improving things and for enhancing the love life you already enjoy. The replies to the tests offer new directions to pursue if you discover an area of ignorance or a lack of expertise.

stamina test

You will prefer to do this in privacy. It looks pretty weird. Get down on your hands and knees and visualize a perfect partner lying beneath you. Take a fix on the time (exactly) from your watch and then move as if you were thrusting into your partner. This is a particularly good exercise for women because it offers firsthand experience of just how full of stamina their men need to be in bed. When you have "screwed" your "partner" for as long as you can possibly manage, check the time on your watch.

how well did you do?

FIVE MINUTES If you are fit, lean, and full of energy you may have managed five minutes or more.

THREE MINUTES This is the time of the average session of sexual intercourse—a timing that hardly sounds like one of the most memorable occasions!

ONE MINUTE OR LESS If, like most women, you have collapsed before one minute is up, you will begin to get an idea of how fit you are—or not.

sexual knowledge test

2

■ Do you know how to:
• Satisfy yourself sexually?
• Satisfy your partner sexually by hand?
• Satisfy your partner sexually with your mouth?

■ Do you know your own erotic hot spots?

■ Do you know your partner's erotic hotspots?

■ Do you know how to perform anal sex so that it feels comfortable?

■ Do you know where your own/your partner's G-spot/prostate is?

■ Do you know how to give a sensual massage?

■ Do you know what is the sexiest time of month for a woman?

■ Do you know what is the sexiest time of the day for a man?

■ Do you know how to:
• Prevent premature ejaculation?
• Overcome impotence difficulties?
• Assist your female partner if she has difficulties reaching orgasm?

■ Have you ever used or would you consider using a sex toy—in particular, a vibrator?

how well did you do?

MORE NO'S If you score more no's than yes's you will realize there are many gaps in your basic sexual knowledge that would benefit from a little sexual education.

MORE YES'S If you scored more yes's than no's, well done! Remember that the wisest among us are those still able to learn. Try some of the sex ideas from the 28-Day Plan.

smoking/drinking test

smoking

DO YOU SMOKE? If so, how many cigarettes a week? And how young were you when you started? The sexual danger for smoking is cumulative. If men smoke heavily during their teens and 20s, they risk developing erectile dysfunction in their 30s and 40s. For women smoking reduces the ability to experience localized sensation in their pelvic area. In addition, the constant wafting of smoke across the face creates wrinkles even faster than prolonged exposure to the sun.

drinking

DO YOU DRINK? If so, how much and how often? A few occasional units of alcohol may lower inhibition and raise feelings of desire. But did you know that alcohol:
• Numbs nerve endings in both male and female genitalia?
• Decreases female lubrication and can lead to painful sex?
• Can depress libido, kill sexual desire, cause impotence?

the manual dexterity test

When you spread out your fingers on a flat tabletop can you:

■ Lift each finger separately up and down, without moving the other fingers and without hesitation?

■ Can you do this first from little finger through to thumb?

■ Can you then do this in reverse—from thumb through to little finger?

■ Finally can you run through the whole hand in both directions without hesitation several times?

The greater manual dexterity you possess, the greater the likelihood that you will be able to play upon your partner's genitals and help them make sexual music.

oral dexterity test

■ Can you move the tip of your tongue up and down rapidly?

■ From side to side rapidly?

■ Can you thrust your tongue forward repeatedly?

If you need an explanation of why this test is useful, there is an important chunk of your sexual knowledge and technique missing.

17

body mass test

This test is a simple matter of measuring your height and then weighing yourself. Work out your body mass from where the line of your weight crosses with the line of your height. The central, darker section of the chart shows the body mass range that counts as healthy. This will be the ideal weight for someone of your height at which to excel at physical exercise, which includes sexual exercise.

body mass index chart

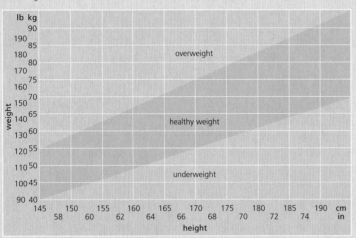

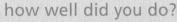

how well did you do?

IF YOU ARE OVER THE IDEAL BODY MASS, this may indicate that you need to lose some weight and generally get more exercise. Men and women who are greatly overweight commonly feel lethargic and lose interest in sex.

IF YOU ARE UNDER THE IDEAL BODY MASS, you may lack stamina and, should you be particularly frail, you may bruise easily. Women who are excessively underweight may miss periods and lose sexual libido.

Note that the chart above only applies to those over 21. If you are below this age, consult your doctor for an indication of your ideal body mass range.

emotional sensitivity test

■ Can you tune in to your partner's mood before you begin to make love?

■ Do you touch, stroke, and hug your partner on occasions other than sex?

■ Do you tell your partner you love him/her at least three times a week?

■ Have you ever made love for your partner's sake even though you have not felt like it?

■ Do you plan (and follow through with) romantic evenings?

■ If circumstances give you little time for romance, do you keep in touch with your lover by phone, letter, and email?

■ Does your partner feel confident enough in his/her relationship with you to say no occasionally? Do you?

■ Do you know what effect your partner's upbringing and early sex experience has had on how they approach sex?

■ Can you communicate difficult sexual requests to your partner?

There are no right or wrong answers. But if you have more no's than yes's, you may want to:
• Learn more about your partner,
• Have more intimate discussions
• Spend enough time on your lover so that he/she feels loved.

final assessment

If you look at what you have learned from doing these tests you now possess some important starting points about your sexual fitness and ability.

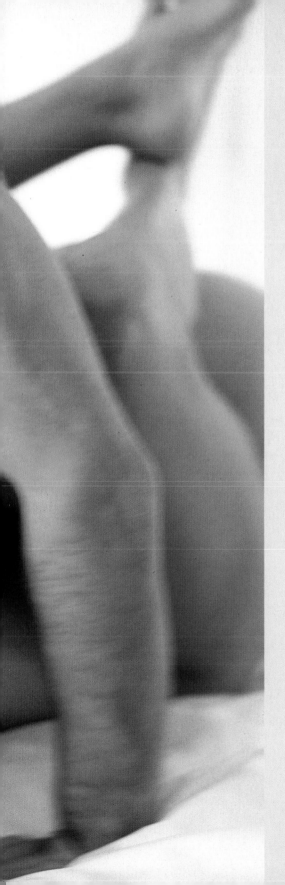

sexercise

FITNESS CERTAINLY isn't everything. But used lovingly and sensuously, it can make you and your partner feel fantastic. And sexual intercourse itself offers wonderful methods of taking aerobic exercise and staying supple! Here we focus on the kind of exercise that facilitates sexual mobility and promotes physical strength. If you can't maintain intercourse for more than three minutes, the sexual experience is unlikely to be satisfactory. Improving sexual strength in no way substitutes for the importance of loving each other or communication, but it helps offer a much better physical experience when you reach the bedroom. On the following pages, you will find exercises that facilitate intercourse and exercises that offer an aerobic type of sexual activity.

balance

A GOOD SENSUAL WORKOUT BEGINS WITH relaxing every muscle in the body. When we come to exercise, we often feel weary. Exhausted people do not perform exercise well. So it is always a good idea to begin with relaxation. Start each workout lying on your back and, working upward through each body part from the toes to the face, clench each muscle one at a time for a count of five, then let go. When you feel ready, move on to the Blood Rush.

blood rush

This exercise develops heat around the head and neck similar to that of sexual arousal. Face each other and hold hands. Let her toes lightly overlap his toes. As he braces himself, she leans back as far as she can safely go and lets her head fall all the way back. This is both disorienting and creates a rush of blood to her head thus facilitating arousal. This exercises muscle groups in the arms of both of you. Hold for a count of 10 before swapping roles. Avoid this exercise if you have shoulder problems.

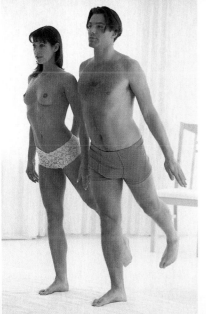

balancing from within

One reason why any sex position works well is because you have developed a strong inner stability. Standing on one leg sounds like a ridiculously simple exercise but unless you have cultivated that inner balance it can be surprisingly difficult to maintain. Start by standing in a balanced way and slowly lift one leg up at the back. Then hold the position, making sure that your pelvis stays level. It helps to remember to draw in your abdominal muscles. If you start to wobble, hold on to something. Do the exercise five times before testing this out on the other foot. Then repeat the exercise, only holding the foot forward instead of backward.

bridge pose

If you can hold this pose for a count of 10 you develop fantastic balance and strength in the forearms, shoulders, and thighs. He lies on his back with his left knee bent, foot on the ground; his right leg lies flat. She lies on top of him on her back, her hands on the ground on each side of his neck, her right leg between his legs and right foot on the ground. Her left leg is slightly raised and bent at the knee. Then she pushes on her hands, straightening her arms, while he pushes her buttocks up so that they are above his pelvis and she is resting on her hands and left foot only. Her bent right leg should be parallel to his bent right leg. In the final position both bodies are virtually symmetrical.

get supple
massage

A KINDER AND GENTLER METHOD of attaining suppleness than stretching is through massage, something that all world-class athletes rely on. The following health massage concentrates on the limbs and waist muscles, on the grounds that these probably do most of the work during sex. The added bonus of a health massage is that if you do it with a lover, you can of course later turn it into something far more erotic. (For further details of sensual massage see pp.98-99.)

arms and legs

Two main massage strokes adequately cover your partner's limbs and reach the musculature that lies beneath the surface. The first is a hand-over-hand pulling technique that uses all the fingers, particularly the thumb, to pull up along the limbs toward the body. Use first one hand, then the other, in small, repetitive pulling strokes to work your way along the arm or leg. Then make a ring of your two hands around your partner's limb and, forming a kind of bracelet, bring that ring up toward the body. You will find you are moving all the tissue underneath your hands and loosening it—something you might do in a lymphatic massage.

muscle movement

Thumb kneeding is a simple, time-honored massage stroke that allows you to probe deeply but gently. Place your thumbs on a muscled area and if you can't find the muscle, push deeply. If you fear hurting your partner, get feedback. Having found a muscle just move the tissue beneath your thumbs, directly over the muscle, in a circular movement. Some people also find using all fingers instead of thumbs alone effective too.

hips and waist

Using the above technique, work from the side of the waist around the top of the buttocks, trying to relax the taut muscles that support the bottom of the spine (see left). When the waist and upper buttock surface has been thoroughly worked, sit on one side of your partner and lean across him/her, placing both hands on the far side of their waist (see right). Pull your partner toward you slightly with one hand, then take the hand off. As their body returns to resting, pull with the other hand and lift off. As you do so, replace the first hand, setting up a continual rocking movement. Work your hands down the sides of the body (the sides of the buttocks) and then back up to the waist.

get supple
stretches

upper thigh stretch

IF YOU'VE EVER MADE LOVE to someone who seemed incapable of bending, whose movements were so stiff you felt like screaming, then you will understand the desirability of becoming supple. Suppleness is what ballet dancers and circus performers aim for. It allows you to perform incredible acts of beauty and athleticism without hurting yourself. And because a dancer knows he can rely on an easy, flexible body, he approaches his routines with a kind of fluid confidence. It's that confidence a really good lover relies on too. Here are some exercises to get you supple and to build your confidence.

Hold on to the back of a chair with one hand, stand upright, and, with the other hand, reach down behind you while bending at the knee and lift the nearest foot up to meet your hand. Grasp the ankle and hold it as close to your upper thigh as your stiff muscles will let you. Make sure that the bent knee is kept close to the standing knee so that, seen from the side, you are standing straight. Keep the knees together. Repeat the stretch with the other leg.

buttock and thigh stretch

Lying on your back, breathe in, and then, on the out-breath, clasp your right knee with both hands and, bending the knee, bring the leg as close to your chest as you can. Hold this stretch for a minute. You should feel the taut muscles on the buttocks and the back of the thigh complain a little. On your next out-breath, let the right leg go back to the floor, keeping your abdominal muscles pulled in. Breathe in, then, on the out-breath, repeat the exercise with the left knee and thigh. Once you are used to the exercise, repeat one leg after the other so that your knees are alternating above you.

inner thigh stretch

Sit on an upright chair, legs as far apart as they will comfortably go. Put your hands on the insides of your thighs and push your legs even farther apart. Feel the inner thigh muscles stretch as you do so. The key is to do the exercise slowly. Sudden pressure might result in an injury.

the *plié*

Opening your inner thigh muscles is essential for traditional intercourse. The *plié* enables you to "turn out" your pelvic muscles as far as possible. Stand side-on to the mirror, one arm resting on the back of a chair. Keeping your balance with the supporting arm, place your feet about six inches apart with toes turned out. Flex at the knees and let yourself bend as far as your legs will comfortably go. You will experience an inclination to lean forward. Resist it. Check in the mirror that as you bend, your torso and head remain upright.

up against a wall

Find a bare wall and wriggle your bottom hard up against it. Then, with your legs high and flat against the wall, let gravity gently part them, taking them as far as they will comfortably go. My former circus-performer trainer gave me a magazine to read and told me to "stay there, girl, for 15 minutes." I didn't think I'd last two but, in spite of the agony, I managed it. Your inner thigh muscles get used to it and allow your legs to shift. My splits were considerably wider after a quarter of an hour. The magazine was good too.

29

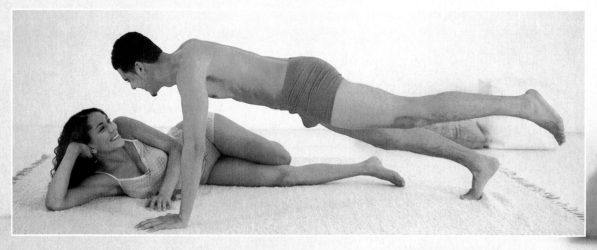

stretching the hips

This exercise allows you to develop arm and shoulder control and strength, while maintaining balance and opening and stretching the hip joint. Support your body on your hands, with your legs out straight behind you. Breathe in and then, on the out-breath, slowly lift one leg up straight behind you. Do not move your hips or arch your back. Breathe in again and then on the out-breath gently lower the leg. Repeat with the other leg. Do the exercise five times with each leg, making sure not to let your body "dip" in the middle.

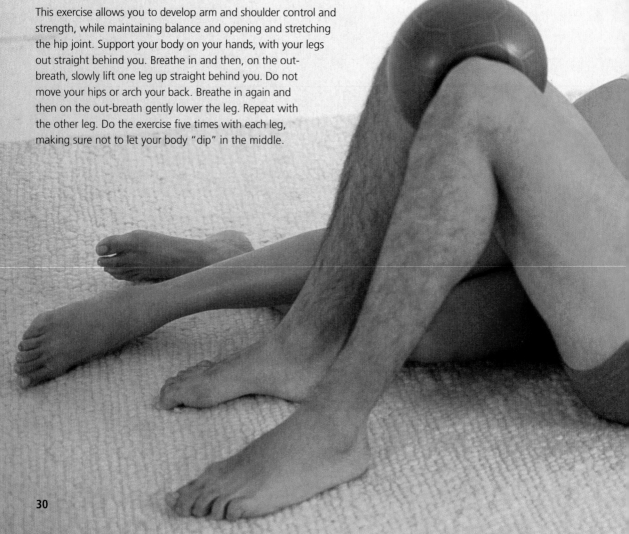

flexible finger exercises

The partner with magic fingers makes a great lover. Standing straight, hold your hands out in front of you, palms down, elbows slightly bent. Ignoring the thumb, separate the first two fingers from the next two, creating a space. Return the fingers to normal. Repeat 10 times. Then, leaving the middle three fingers together, separate the thumb and fifth finger, stretching these hard. Repeat 10 times.

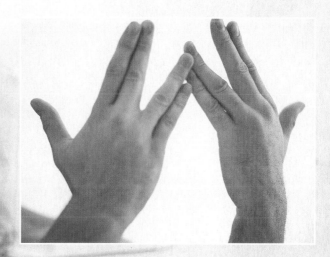

extra thigh flex

If your thighs can take the strain, you'll be able to make love for longer. Lie on your back with your knees bent and your head supported by a small pillow. Place a Pilates ball between your knees and squeeze, then release, making sure not to drop the ball. Repeat 20 times.

get supple
stability

IF YOU'VE EVER BEEN CURIOUS ENOUGH to touch or handle a snake you'll know that its body is hard, full of taut muscles that allow it to undulate across the ground at (sometimes) frightening speeds. Men and women often move in an undulating movement, lovingly writhing above or below their partner. That is, they do if they are in reasonably good shape. A Pilates teacher would tell you that if you want to move with controlled strength in bed you need that bedrock of Pilates discipline—core stability.

Core stability comes from having superb control of your abdominal muscles. Most of the early Pilates exercises focus on tightening up these muscles so that you can be completely still and balanced from your middle even though your arms, legs, and torso are undergoing the most complicated contortions.

So for those of you who want to feel you have complete control of any movement that sexual intercourse requires, here are two basic exercises that allow you to develop core stability.

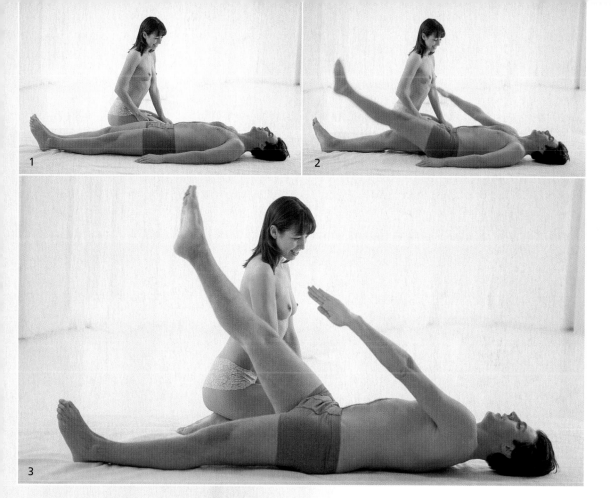

limb raises

Lie on your back with your legs straight and your arms by the side of your body (1). Breathe in. On the out-breath pull in your abdominal muscles while, at the same time, lifting the right arm, right shoulder, and left leg (2). On the in-breath lower the limbs. Repeat the exercise several times and then do it with the other side (3). Keep an eye on your midsection. As you lift your limbs, the muscles in your abdomen should remain taut and drawn in. You will find that the steadiness of your abdomen allows you to perform the lifting easily.

stomach crunch

Lie on your back with your knees bent and your hands clasped behind your head, elbows out to the side. Breathe in; then, on the out-breath, pull in your abdominal muscles and at the same time tuck your chin in a little while pulling up slightly with your arms and head. Your head and arms are now off the ground but your shoulders remain touching the floor. Your abdomen should remain low and taut. Breathe in and let your arms and head drop gradually back to the floor. Repeat the sequence 10 times.

pleasure
fitness

SOME COUPLES LOVE doing everything together and working out is usually high on the list of shared activities. If you exercise together try doing at least part of it naked. When you're naked you can see which parts of your body are lithe and supple and which are chunky and inflexible.

There is, however, a deeper aspect to shared exercise, which is the issue of trust. If you are dependent on your lover to hold you and not drop you, you need faith in his/her nurturing ability, not to mention his/her strength. On this and following pages you will find exercises to do together. Many of these can easily be adapted to do on your own.

freeing the pelvic girdle

This is based on an exercise Betty Dodson gave her Bodysex students in the exotic days of the 1970s when she was inventing her particular form of liberating sexuality. You need dance music with a good beat. The man stands behind his partner with his hands on her hips. She begins to circle her hips to the music as if she were hoola-hooping and he helps her movements by moving her hips manually. Once she has the rhythm down, he then moves closer and copies her circling so that the pair circles in unison.

back arch

Many people find that this exercise alleviates back pain, but if you have any anxieties about a back condition skip this one or do it with extreme care. Get on your hands and knees with your weight evenly distributed, hands just below the shoulders, fingers pointing forward and knees slightly apart. Gaze downward; your head should be in line with your spine. Breathe in and then, on the out-breath, pull your abdomen muscles up toward your spine, while at the same time arching your back so that you look a little like an angry cat. Hold for around 10 seconds and then relax.

the roll-up

This simple Pilates exercise frees the back from stiffness. Start by standing side-on to the mirror. Breathe in. On the out-breath, pull in your abdominal muscles and very slowly allow your head to drop forward and down so that your spine bends very gradually and your arms reach toward the floor. It's helpful to imagine your spine actually uncurling, each vertebra unlocking and moving forward. Your abdomen stays upright for as long as possible before you tilt from the hips. Some people can reach as far as the floor, even placing their hands flat, but this is not necessary. The real goal of the exercise is to achieve the sense of curling and uncurling the spine.

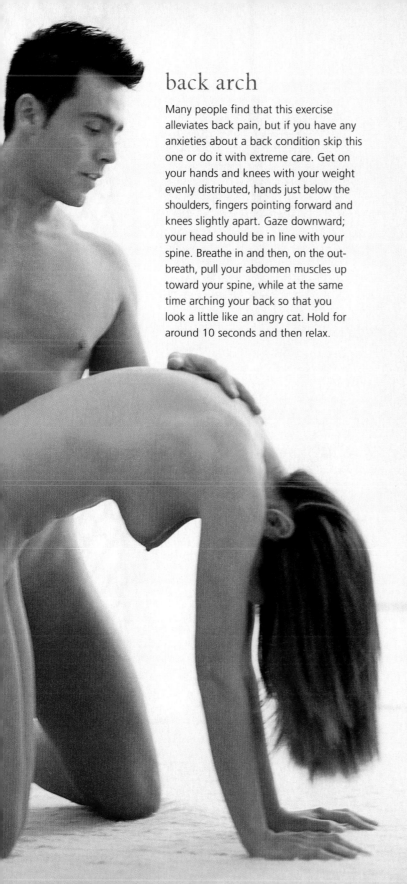

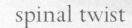

spinal twist

This is a great stretch for the abdominal and waist muscles. Lie on your back with your knees drawn up, feet flat on the ground. With arms out at the sides (and head supported by a pillow) breathe in. On the out-breath let your knees slowly fall to one side while your head turns to the opposite side. Breathe in again and on the next out-breath let your strong abdominal muscles "pull" your legs up again to the start position while your head also moves back. Then repeat on the other side. Repeat the whole exercise several times.

lion stretch

This is a fun stretch to do together. Start by lying on your stomach head to head, then slowly raise yourself on your arms. If you can, fully extend the arms, so that the elbows lock. Keep your hips in contact with the floor. You should feel the stretch in the lower back and at the front of the abdomen. Vary the stretch by opening your mouth wide and sticking out your tongue; this will tone your facial muscles and probably make your partner laugh.

37

body pride

THERE'S A STORY TOLD by Clare Rayner, an advice columnist in the UK famous for her big personality and big body shape. She describes how she came across some old photographs of herself in her early 20s and realized, belatedly, how beautiful she had looked then. Yet, she also ruefully remembered that when she was young she felt terrible about her appearance, always thinking she was fat and unattractive. Clare's story has always seemed to me to be a moral tale—one about learning to love yourself. The New York sex guru Betty Dodson also tells the story of how, as a young adolescent, she had found her developing genitals incredibly ugly, a view encouraged by the secretive atmosphere surrounding sex in the US of the 1940s. It was only in her sixties that Betty began to see her genitals as beautiful. Hopefully you will feel better about your appearance after reading this book, and here are a couple of exercises to help you on your way.

"The message of this book is to get into healthy shape, be it big or small, but to feel fit and well with it. The better men and women feel about their bodies, the better too they feel about sex."

mirror exercise

Stand naked before a full-length mirror and tell yourself first what you love about your body and then what you love about your genitals. Do NOT dwell on what you dislike—this is an exercise in positivity.

partner exercise

Stand naked with your partner and tell each other what you love about each other. No criticisms or disparagements are allowed, only positive, admiring statements. It's really amazing how good you feel after appreciation of this kind, even if the exercise might appear somewhat artificial.

get fit
through sex

I WHOLEHEARTEDLY BELIEVE THAT SEX should be done because you love and are deeply attracted to a partner and not just for mundane reasons such as streamlining the body. But vigorous sexual activity undoubtedly counts as aerobic activity, provided that it goes on long enough. Different types of sexual activity strengthen different muscle groups, expand the lungs, and oxygenate the body. In other words, sex can be physically good for you, in addition to offering the better-known benefit of sensual pleasure.

On the following pages I outline some of the more athletic sexual positions, to be tried slowly, carefully—and sensually! We start with the more athletic positions for her, before moving on to the more common missionary positions (for these see pp.48-53).

woman-on-top

Any woman who has moved on top of her man to give him as fast and as vigorous an experience as possible will testify that this can be extremely stimulating, but also very tiring. The advantage for the woman of being on top is that she can vary her position. She might prefer to thrust with her body close up against his, or alternatively from an upright position. She may want to focus on his sensation or she may want to use this position to satisfy herself. It also allows the woman to slow down the lovemaking if she senses that her partner is getting dangerously near the "point of no return" before she is ready.

rear-entry woman on top

This stroke can be surprisingly sensual since the thrust of intercourse is experienced throughout the whole of the woman's buttocks. For the man it contains the element of surprise by being quite simply, an unusual position in which to make love. To get into this position the man should lie on his back, while the woman sits astride him, facing his feet. She guides his erect penis into her and then leans back and supports herself with her arms. Her movements form a sexual version of the bridge pose (see p.23). The stroke takes a lot of suppleness, flexibility of hips, and strength in the arms. Alternatively, if it is too backbreaking, the woman can sit upright and, using her feet for balance, lean forward slightly to give her an easier thrust.

kama sutra
elephant posture

This rear-entry position has the woman lying face downward with her legs slightly open. Her man kneels between her legs and enters her from behind, then leans forward and over her body, supporting himself on his arms. Although his pelvis pivots on her buttocks, core abdominal muscles and hip flexors are exercised.

This variation of the elephant posture (right) offers a less athletic, but more intimate position for lovemaking. The man rests on his elbows and forearms, while keeping the entire length of his torso in intimate contact with his partner.

combining positions

Standing postures include some of the more athletic positions for sex. These usually involve the man leaning back against a hard surface with the woman leaning forward on to him. He half-lifts his partner toward, then away from, him to allow for satisfactory thrusting. Exhausting as it can be, a position like the Suspended Congress (opposite) might be followed by the much gentler position below, which allows for more prolonged lovemaking.

side-by-side clasping

Perhaps as an antidote to the Suspended Congress, this position makes sex feel far less stressed and strained. It allows a couple to show their loving emotion and gives them easy face-to-face contact for kissing and murmuring words of love. It also ensures that they use hip and buttock thrusts, strengthening muscles in both the buttocks and the upper thighs. Lovemaking tends to be easier if the couple take turns moving.

the suspended congress

The most challenging standing sex position is this *Kama Sutra* pose that emulates the extraordinary erotic carvings seen on the side of ancient Indian temple walls. The man leans against a wall, the woman puts her arms around his neck, and he lifts her by holding her thighs or by locking his hands underneath her buttocks. He then moves her backward and forward. She grips him around the hips with her knees and pushes off against the wall when appropriate. The position encourages the development of her full arm and shoulder muscles plus truly taut hip muscles. It also develops his arm and abdominal strength.

the three-handed massage

As a reward for all the previous sexercise, the three-handed massage is perfect. On one level it continues the aerobic workout, while on another it offers a unique sensual experience. The massage can be given by either man or woman but when one partner is substantially heavier than the other, care needs to be taken while sitting astride him/her.

2 After massaging for 15 minutes or so seated upright, lean forward and let your chest do some massaging of its own, while continuing to work on his/her shoulders with your hands. If he has a hairy chest he will need extra oil here to prevent painful hair-pulling. After a while, let your genitals slide slowly and gently across your partner's genitals and let them massage too while your hands continue elsewhere.

1 Begin with one partner lying on his/her back and oil his/her body with a liberal amount of lubrication, especially around the hips, pelvis, and genitals. Then sit astride his/her abdomen. Begin by massaging the chest, arms, and shoulders, then lean back to massage as much of the thighs and legs as you can reach. You might incorporate some of the arm and leg massage described earlier (see pp.24-25). Use plenty of massage oil so that his/her body becomes slippery. And make a point of sliding around on the abdomen as you work. There should be enough oil to allow you to do this.

3 Take things slowly and when the arousal is enough, gently ease yourselves into intercourse, moving slowly and lightly just as if you were continuing the massage. The ultimate goal is to massage both inside (or around) your partner's genitals while also massaging the rest of the body. The process is a gradual, subtle one, with the massage gaining an extra dimension, the genitals offering a third hand to assist the first two in their sensual gift.

fittest missionary

By now everyone must know that the Missionary Position acquired its name from the antics of a proselytizing couple who were spied on by the natives as they were enjoying the pleasure God had sent them. The natives, possibly more athletic than the Europeans, were interested and amused by the man-on-top position that the traveling ministers tended to adopt with their wives. At least, that's the myth.

For everyone who laughs at the basic man-on-top love position there are many more of us who value it. It does, after all, have a pretty good track record of allowing us to experience deep satisfaction. And it's no accident that so many of us naturally make love like this. And aside from the physical practicalities, (the man has tended to be stronger than the woman and is therefore more able to bear his weight on his arms and legs as he thrusts) the face-to-face alliance means that a loving couple can kiss and see their partner's arousal. The Missionary allows us to develop feelings of love and intimacy over and above the sexual activity. And such is the success of the position that

there have been many variations on it, allowing the man to thrust more deeply, or the woman to position her clitoris higher. On the next few pages I outline a few easy exercises, which make these variations more successful.

classic missionary

The missionary is a man-on-top position where the man lies between his woman's outspread legs (slightly drawn up). Supporting his weight on hands or elbows, he thrusts into her vagina. Add to this kissing and nuzzling and you get a very tasty position.

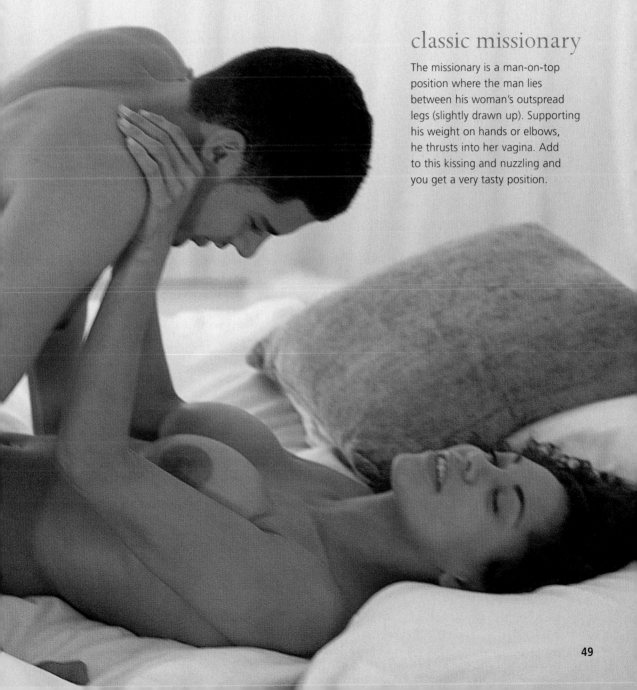

deep missionary

One variation that alters the sensation for both man and woman is the Deep Missionary Position. This is where, by moving her feet, the woman subtly changes the sexual experience.

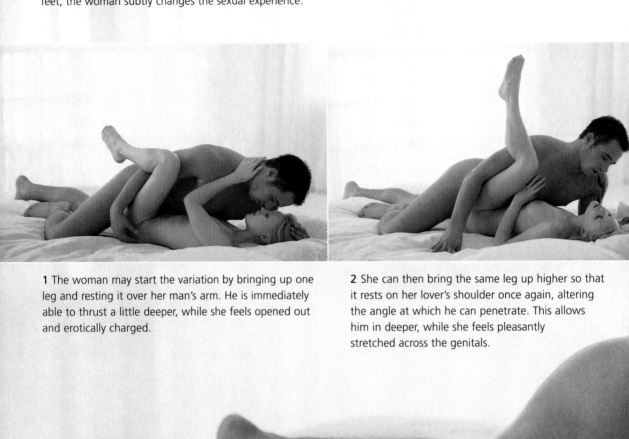

1 The woman may start the variation by bringing up one leg and resting it over her man's arm. He is immediately able to thrust a little deeper, while she feels opened out and erotically charged.

2 She can then bring the same leg up higher so that it rests on her lover's shoulder once again, altering the angle at which he can penetrate. This allows him in deeper, while she feels pleasantly stretched across the genitals.

3 Finally, she brings her legs up high and rests them over her partner's shoulders. This allows her man seriously deep penetration, although it may not do a great deal for her.

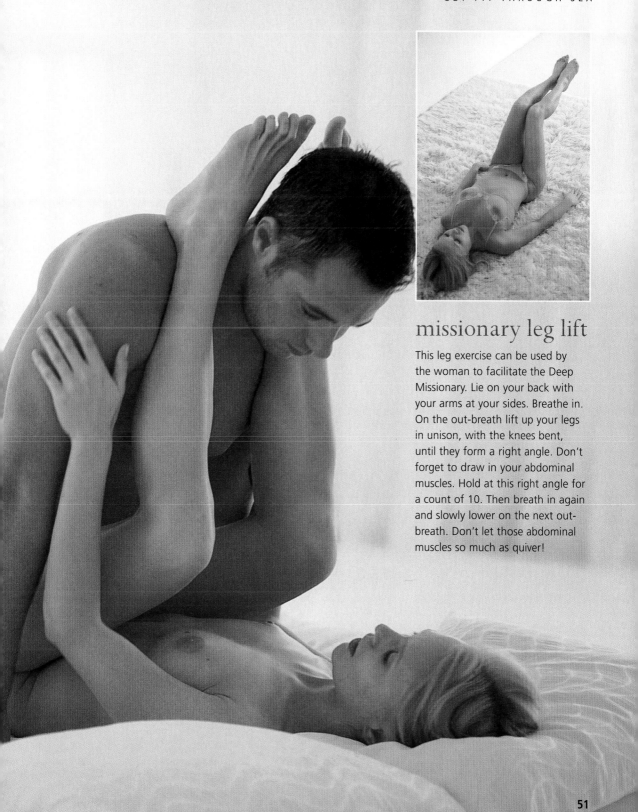

missionary leg lift

This leg exercise can be used by the woman to facilitate the Deep Missionary. Lie on your back with your arms at your sides. Breathe in. On the out-breath lift up your legs in unison, with the knees bent, until they form a right angle. Don't forget to draw in your abdominal muscles. Hold at this right angle for a count of 10. Then breath in again and slowly lower on the next out-breath. Don't let those abdominal muscles so much as quiver!

best missionary

One of the snags about the Missionary Position is that most of the action is made by the man. If you're the woman, this can feel frustrating—despite the undoubtedly good sensation of face-to-face intercourse. But there are a couple of variations besides waving your legs in the air that can substantially change the basic moves of this position.

bundle exercise

To help you with the position to the right there is a classic Pilates move normally used to relieve aches and pains in the body after exercise. You lie on your back, draw your legs up, knees bent, and clasp them around the outside with your arms, at the same time bringing your head up slightly, off the floor. Hold for a couple of seconds and then relax. Repeat five times. The exercise opens up the vertebrae and stretches the back.

go to meet him

With feet on the ground and knees bent, the woman raises her pelvis and therefore thrusts part of the way up as he thrusts down. It is a difficult position to sustain with the hips raised, so to make the thrusting truly satisfying practice core balance control (see pp.22-23). A strong abdomen and fit back muscles are also vital here (see pp.32-33 for specific exercises).

wrap him up

In this variation the woman wraps her legs around her lover's waist, without lifting her bottom up. This opens her pelvis wider, while simultaneously working the thigh muscles.

"The Missionary allows us to develop feelings of love and intimacy over and above the sexual activity."

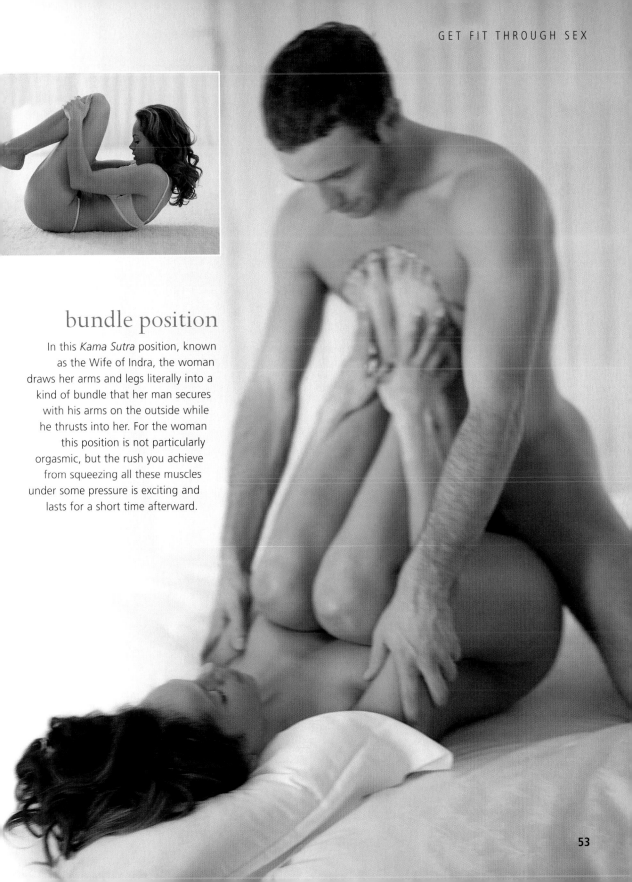

bundle position

In this *Kama Sutra* position, known as the Wife of Indra, the woman draws her arms and legs literally into a kind of bundle that her man secures with his arms on the outside while he thrusts into her. For the woman this position is not particularly orgasmic, but the rush you achieve from squeezing all these muscles under some pressure is exciting and lasts for a short time afterward.

turning position

The *Kama Sutra* Turning Position has long been one of
the most challenging to perform. It consists of the man
turning in a complete circle above his partner during
intercourse and never once losing penetration. In order
to manage this, without breaking off genital contact,
the man needs to possess strong arms and thighs,
which are capable of taking his weight as he maneuvers.
Incidentally, the roles of this position can easily be
reversed, with the woman sitting on top of the man's
penis. During lovemaking, varying positions in this way
can be used to increase the feeling of closeness. As the
man moves around in the turning position, his partner
can demonstrate her tenderness by embracing or
caressing his back, shoulders, and sides. Another
movement involves raising a leg slightly and hold
it straight and firm as it swings across the partner's
body. Muscle control needs to be good here, practice
holding your leg up to achieve this.

sexual stamina

HAVING TRIED OUT an assortment of sexual positions, you have tested what you and your body are presently capable of. You should have an excellent idea of what you can manage easily and when you need to produce that little bit extra to keep things going. The little extra is called stamina and it often makes sex more pleasurable.

Why? Because the most intense sexual sensation happens over a long buildup of sexual excitement and tension by stimulating each other in every way you can imagine. And for this you need to be able to last during lovemaking.

the squeeze

When the man is about to reach that "point of no return" firmly squeeze the head of the penis, just below the coronal ridge, between finger or thumb. This can be done by either of you. After this, the erection tends to deflate somewhat. That is fine, since it allows the woman the time to "catch up" with the man.

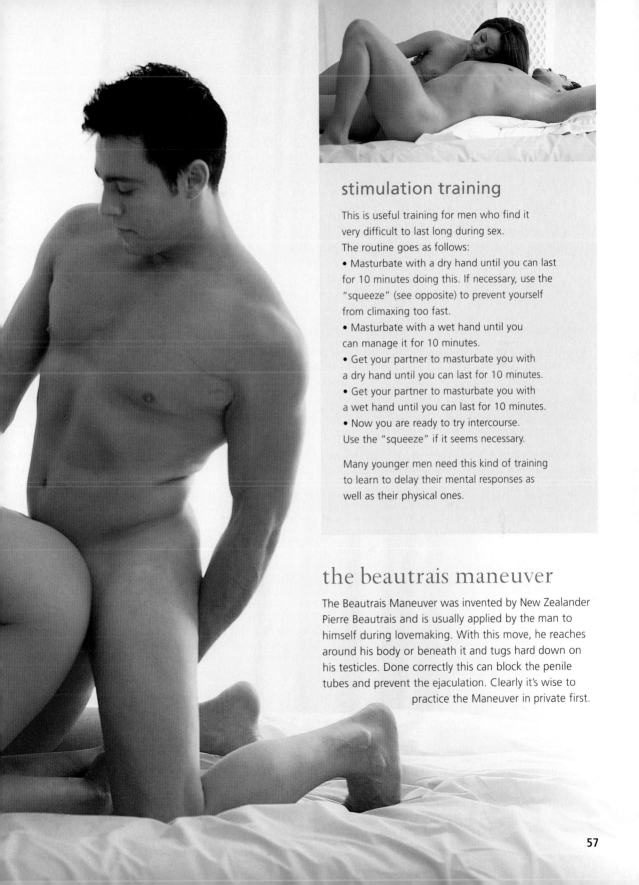

stimulation training

This is useful training for men who find it very difficult to last long during sex. The routine goes as follows:

• Masturbate with a dry hand until you can last for 10 minutes doing this. If necessary, use the "squeeze" (see opposite) to prevent yourself from climaxing too fast.

• Masturbate with a wet hand until you can manage it for 10 minutes.

• Get your partner to masturbate you with a dry hand until you can last for 10 minutes.

• Get your partner to masturbate you with a wet hand until you can last for 10 minutes.

• Now you are ready to try intercourse. Use the "squeeze" if it seems necessary.

Many younger men need this kind of training to learn to delay their mental responses as well as their physical ones.

the beautrais maneuver

The Beautrais Maneuver was invented by New Zealander Pierre Beautrais and is usually applied by the man to himself during lovemaking. With this move, he reaches around his body or beneath it and tugs hard down on his testicles. Done correctly this can block the penile tubes and prevent the ejaculation. Clearly it's wise to practice the Maneuver in private first.

eat for sex

IN ORDER to maintain a supple body, fit for sex, you need to pay attention to two main areas of body maintenance. The first is adequate movement and exercise, the second, which is equally as important, is a healthy diet. This does not necessarily mean you need to lose weight but it does mean you need to be aware of how body size and shape affect your options where mobility is concerned. On the following pages I describe the kind of food that promotes good sexual health, empowering you with enough energy and vitality enabling you to move on to the ultimate plan for body maintenance – the 28-Day Plan itself.

the
sensual
picnic

Foods can be suggestive. They put ideas in our head. They do this through their appearance, their texture, the way they feel, and the way they taste as they slip down our throats. Sex gurus have always known it. Here are some food ideas for fun lovemaking.

the visual feast

Prepare a huge platter of exquisitely prepared exotic fruits, exotically laid out, juicy and colorful. Offer it to your partner as he/she takes a foamy sweet-smelling bath and insist on feeding them in between soaping their body with your exploratory hands. As he/she lies back and enjoys the heat, the scent and the gorgeous appearance of the fruit, tilt a champagne flute to their mouth but deliberately let some of it spill down their naked body across the chest and into the water. Food and drink here form part of an overall sensual treat. After drying your partner off in fluffy, heated towels lead him/her off for a massage.

secret dining

Make sure that the setting for your picnic is private and definitely not overlooked. Pack the picnic hamper with foods that you crunch or lick such as celery and lollipops. Try bringing some frozen grapes (in a thermos flask) and eat first the grapes then take a mouthful of a hot drink, then go for another grape, alternating the sensations of hot and cold. Share the same piece of watermelon and let your mouths meet in the middle. If you want to seem sophisticated and expensive, serve blinis (tiny pancakes) with caviar and sour cream. Eat the food as provocatively as you can, make your picnic suggestive.

erotic foods

Peaches They taste sweet and refreshing with an appearance that is tastily suggestive. The smooth blush of a rounded peach looks a lot like the downy cheeks of a beautiful woman. Peaches contain high levels of vitamins A and C (ascorbic acid) and potassium, great for cold prevention and glowing good health.

Banana The banana's phallic shape is certainly in part responsible for its popularity as an aphrodisiac. But from a scientific standpoint, bananas offer a bountiful source of potassium and B-complex vitamins, both vital elements in sex hormone production. Banana blossom also appears in Filipino recipes as an aphrodisiac

rude food

Use a paintbrush to paint your lover's erogenous zones with cream and honey, then lick it off. Decorate your partner's body with food substances, photograph your masterpiece, then proceed to eat it. Copy the popular ice-cream advertisements and feed each other spoonfuls of the cold, slippery stuff, while naked. Occasionally let a chunk of "gelato" travel down his/her chest or pelvis. The careless feeder is then forced to lick their partner clean.

"Don't forget: good sex needs plenty of energy. Raw food contains far more minerals and vitamins than cooked food."

Chocolate The Aztecs referred to chocolate as "nourishment of the Gods". Chocolate contains PEA (phenylethylamine), which is also the chemical we naturally secrete when we fall in love. It's the chemical that gives us the love-high and helps us bond in the first place. It also contains natural ingredients that cause the brain to release serotonin, a hormone responsible for feelings of relaxation and pleasure. As a neat bonus, chocolate contains more antioxidant (a substance that prevents cancer) than red wine. Chocolate that contains a higher quantity of cocoa is purportedly a more effective aphrodisiac, so choose dark chocolate over its lighter cousins.

Caviar Caviar is considered by the Russians to be aphrodisiac; it does contain many important minerals and omega 3 oils, which help regulate blood clotting, blood pressure, and boost immunity to disease. The rarity, price, and snob value may be more of a turn-on than the roe itself.

Champagne White wine isn't as good for you as the deep red variety, but what it loses in health benefits it more than makes up in aphrodisiac effect. Champagne brings on a sexy high faster than most other alcoholic drinks, the bubbles in sparkling wine make the alcohol enter our system more quickly. Remember though, if you drink too much of it, your performance will wane. You have been warned!

Figs An open fig is thought to emulate the female sex organs and traditionally thought of as a sexual stimulant. A man breaking

open a fig and eating it in front of his lover is carrying out a powerfully erotic act.

Pine nuts Zinc is a key mineral necessary to maintain male potency and pine nuts are rich in zinc. There are records of pine nuts being used to stimulate the libido as far back as medieval times.

Pineapple Rich in vitamin C and and used in the homeopathic treatment for impotence. Add a spear to a sweet rum drink for a tasty prelude to an evening of passion.

Raspberries and strawberries Perfect foods for hand feeding your lover. They invite love and are described in erotic literature as "fruit nipples". Both are high in vitamin C and make a sweet, light dessert.

Asparagus Asparagus is a miracle food, so laden with medicinal properties that you will see it mentioned in two different sections in this book. It contains

substances that act as a diuretic, it neutralizes ammonia (which makes us tired) and protects small blood vessels from rupturing. In other words it helps us stay thin, boosts our energy, and protects us during moments of high passion. With its bold spear-like shape, asparagus is wickedly suggestive and has clearly gained its amatory reputation from its appearance. It also contains good amounts of vitamins A and C.

Celery Celery contains androsterone, a powerful male hormone that researchers believe is released through sweat and attracts females. This is a great way to get your daily allowance of greens, guys!

Vanilla The brain recognises scent in the hypothalamus, a gland that controls memory and emotion. Pleasing scents in food – such as the fragrance of vanilla – have a powerful effect on the sex drive.

foods to lift the libido

The *Kama Sutra* nurtured many poisonous-sounding concoctions that were supposed to prevent impotence. The ancient Egyptians swore by the blue lotus flower. A recent nutritional analysis of the lotus found that the roots of the plant do indeed contain substances analogous to those in ginseng and that, therefore, it might have contributed (in some small way) to Cleopatra's sexual energy levels!

YOUR LIBIDO-LIFTING SHOPPING CART today might contain certain seeds and pulses known to contain phytoestrogens, good for women's sexual health and helpful in lowering cholesterol levels. Ask at your health food store for recommendations. You can bake seeds into bread and cakes and remain healthy and youthful well into your sixties as a result of eating them.

fabulous foods

Asparagus An ideal source of fiber, asparagus helps regulate intestinal function. It is packed with vitamins A, B1, B2, and C, minerals such as calcium, copper, and phosphorous, and essential amino acids. Asparagus also has diuretic properties, making it beneficial for kidney function, and a valuable aid to dieters. Again, we return to the notion that a healthy lover is one who maintains a healthy digestive system and asparagus helps us to do this by clearing waste from the body's system and leaving us thin and energetic. Recent studies have found that an asparagus extract also has a beneficial action on the heart muscle—and a slight sedative/relaxing effect, making it an ideal food to calm tense nerves.

Avocado Despite the avocado's similarity, when halved, to the female genitalia, the Aztecs called the avocado "Ahuacuatl," which translated means "testicle tree," believing this fruit, which hangs in pairs, to resemble them in shape. Avocado is rich in vitamin E, a substance that nurtures the smoothness and health of your skin. It is particularly valuable to help scars heal and since it is through the skin that we experience sensuality, it's important that we have a regular supply of vitamin E. And eating avocados is a particularly attractive method of absorbing it.

Cardamom The little black seeds of cardamom contain not only two androgens (the hormones that increase sexual desire in men) but also cineole, a compound known to stimulate the central nervous system.

Ginger A close relative of cardamom, ginger is the natural world's Viagra. I only discovered this recently, long after I took

a legacy of the
kama sutra

An ancient recipe was entitled *How to Sleep with Countless Women*. The cook was advised to crush together shringataka (not the yoga regimen!), jasmine, and wild fig with liquorice, sugar, and milk. Cook the mixture over a low fire with clarified butter (ghee) before dividing it into cakes. Eat the cakes, advised the author of the *Kama Sutra*, and you'll be sleeping with hordes of women. The figs and liquorice were likely to purge the body of waste matter, so perhaps the male in question seemed thin and fit and therefore devastatingly attractive as a result!

to putting a slice in my early-morning hot water and lemon. True, I had been feeling a warm glow, but hadn't made the connection. Fortunately scientists now have!

Ginseng Ginseng is an "adaptogen," a phrase used by herbalists to refer to a plant that helps the body adapt to physical and mental stress (perhaps by affecting hormone levels), by stimulating the body when it's run down, or relaxing the body when it's stressed. It is believed that ginseng's ability to alleviate fatigue involves the modulation of the hypothalamic-pituitary-adrenal axis (HPA). This can induce the secretion of adrenocorticotropic hormones, helping the body withstand heat, cold, infection, and other physical stresses. The active compounds in ginseng are substances called "ginsenosides." There are some instances where ginseng should be taken with caution, or not taken at all, due to a possible reduction in blood sugar. Those taking diabetic medication or anticoagulants should avoid ginseng, as should pregnant women and women with unstable hormone cycles.

Oats It may not be an accident that the phrase "sowing your wild oats" has slipped into our vocabulary. It seems as though there's more to breakfast than previously met the eye. The alleged aphrodisiac "avena sativa" turns out to be an extract from oats straw. Avena sativa is said to free up bound testosterone in both men and women. Most positive effects of testosterone, including sex drive, are attributed to free testosterone. Too much bound testosterone contributes to a lower sex drive. Try raw rolled oats as a dessert, combined with a few sweet raspberries, brown sugar, and milk.

Oily fish Oily fish, such as salmon, tuna, shark, eel, herring, mackerel, and sardines, and many forms of white fish, including sole and turbot, contain phosphorus, calcium, vitamins A, B, and D, and omega oils that lower cholesterol levels and keep arteries clear. Sexual arousal depends on a good blood supply. Aging can lead to the narrowing of arteries and blood supply can become restricted by furred artieries. An efficient blood supply is directly responsible for sensation in both the penis and vagina. So eating your weekly supply of oily fish can help safeguard sexual arousal.

Shellfish All shellfish contain phosphorus, calcium, iodine, iron, vitamin B, and glycophosphates, essentials for strength and health.

Tomatoes Tomatoes are rich in the phytochemical lycopene, which can help prevent prostate cancer. And in case you think prostate cancer only happens to older men, think again. Even men of 23 have been known to develop it. Like most other vegetables, these days most tomatoes are intensively farmed and may be covered in pesticide, so make sure you scrub them well before eating.

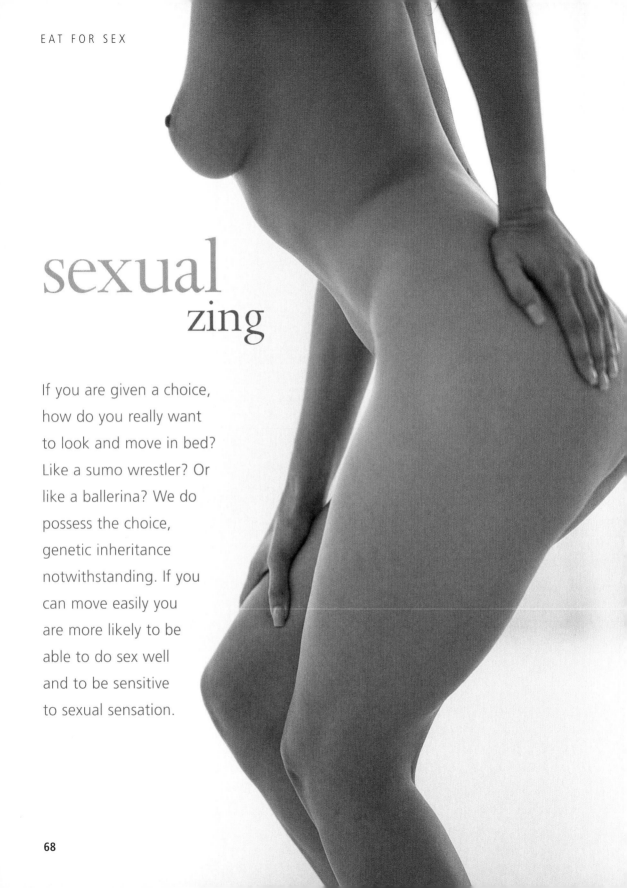

sexual
zing

If you are given a choice, how do you really want to look and move in bed? Like a sumo wrestler? Or like a ballerina? We do possess the choice, genetic inheritance notwithstanding. If you can move easily you are more likely to be able to do sex well and to be sensitive to sexual sensation.

you are what you eat

New York sex guru Betty Dodson used to teach that a little fasting was good for you and that in order to aid digestion you might take time out (say three or four days) to eat your food in the form of blended juices. The result when you did this was that you looked thin, felt fit, and could move like a dancer. Movement was big with Betty. She felt that if you couldn't move easily you were unlikely to be able to do sex well or to be especially sensitive to sexual sensation. Since Betty was a miracle of quick, lithe attractiveness and so too was her assistant Sheila Shea, it was easy to believe in her approach.

the inner you

In order to look like a dancer you need to think about the effect that food has on the interior of your body and on your digestion in particular. Everyone differs in what this consists of. I find that bread bloats me, which is tough because I like it. But I have quickly learned to respond to signals my stomach sends out in the form of pain. I check what I have just eaten and make a mental note to either eat less of it in future or cut it out altogether.

What does bad digestion consist of? Anything that causes your stomach pain. And why does this matter? It matters because it is very difficult to be brilliant in bed if your digestive system is in agony. So investigate what food substances make you suffer. Onions, garlic, strong spices, cream, cinnamon, to name but a few popular foods: all taste delicious but are capable of causing awful internal discomfort.

purify!

Eliminating painful foods is not the only route to good digestion. You also need to unclog the inner you. Think Princess Di. The Princess was famous for aerobic activity, her careful diet, and her courage to experiment with such aids to digestion as a high colonic. Whatever you think of the latter you have to admit that the Princess was a picture of glowing health.

The body is a system to purify. Send through plain liquids, green vegetables, fresh fruit. Liquid and fiber clean out the colon. If there are any problems here go for citrus fruit first thing, make big with the prunes, and cut out most (but not all) fats and carbohydrates. Cut out unnecessary sugar, especially in cakes and cookies. Buy canned fruit in juice, not syrup. Minimizing your sugar intake will rid your system of candida, something that in the 21st century most of us suffer from. Candida feeds on sugar. When you see models in those skimpy underwear ads, baring their clear, spotless buttocks, you can be sure that sugar does not figure in their diet.

Discover what your painful foods are by:

- eliminating suspect foods for a while
- noting if there is any difference
- and then reintroducing them.

If your digestion reacts badly immediately, then it's pretty clear these are poor foods for you. The first week of my 28-Day Plan starts by eliminating these foods so that you can find out for yourself what affects your digestion. You then reintroduce them in successive weeks to evaluate their effect on you.

digestive enzymes

Pineapple, mango, and papaya are crammed full of special digestive enzymes that allow your stomach acids to work efficiently processing food. Native Brazilians believe you should eat the small black seeds found in the center of the papaya on the grounds that they cleanse the inner you. You can make a great smoothie from these fruits that gives an early-morning boost to your digestion

In addition, those with serious stomach difficulties should consider eating live yogurt containing fresh lacto-bacillus on a daily basis. This provides natural relief from stomach pain.

eating in the raw

Why eat raw plain food? Because raw food retains the natural vitamins and minerals that cooking often destroys. Eating raw food daily provides us with vital nutrients, while at the same time offering enough roughage to facilitate the easiest and most rapid expulsion of digestive waste. Even during winter, one meal a day should consist of raw leaves, sprouts, and shoots. In fact, especially during winter, when our skins will be starved of sunlight and vital vitamins as a result. Incidentally, the canning process removes many of the vitamins and minerals that vegetables and fruit naturally contain. It's best to eat fresh.

sex diet intensive

The 28-Day Plan (see pp.78-145) has been designed with sexual well-being in mind. In the first week you cut out all food substances that might cause painful or even allergic reactions. In the second you continue to cut out such substances but add certain foods that cleanse the inner organs and facilitate waste expulsion. In the third week a few of the "forbidden" foods are reintroduced, one-by-one, to find out what reaction you have to them. In the fourth week you establish a healthy permanent food regimen, preferably to be followed forever. This is not a weight-loss diet, but one to specifically reduce abdominal bloating and relieve sluggishness. Combine the diet with sexercise for maximum effect.

painful foods

Everyone has different reactions to different foods. Manna to one may be poison to another. Try eliminating, then reintroducing, these foods to gauge your own digestive response.

Broccoli Dripping with antioxidant that reduces signs of aging. A few people react with abdominal wind.
Brussel sprouts Full of vitamins but can also cause flatulence.
Cabbage Acts as a diuretic, is invaluable as a diet ingredient, but causes flatulence for a few.
Carrots Full of beta-carotene and less likely to be painful.
Cauliflower Also known to cause flatulence for some.
Celery Less likely to create a reaction. Great for sexual energy.
Chilli Adored by some, feared by others. Chilli can actually blister people whose skins are especially sensitive to it.
Citrus fruits A fantastic aid to digestion and recommended as a breakfast food. Those with stomach ulcers may find them acidic.
Garlic An essential aid to food flavoring but, sadly, not tolerated by everyone. Used universally to stave off colds but too much of it can also stave off people!
Melon Many people believe it should be eaten on its own and not with a meal, on the grounds that it can conflict with other foods and make digestion painful.
Mushrooms Regarded as an aphrodisiac since early days, but to be avoided by those with candida.
Onions Cause an allergic reaction with some.

sex
snacks

Hunger often adds a
sharpness and clarity
to sexual experience.

BETTY DODSON, famous New York sex guru, used to teach her
students a unique method of sex snacking. "Instead of making
straight for the ice box for an ice-cream when you come in
from work, at the time of the day when you are most low in
energy and starving for a sugar-high, steer past it and head for
the bedroom." In the bedroom, Betty exhorted, you should
give yourself a wonderful treat in the shape of a rewarding
session with your vibrator.

Betty didn't know it but she was advocating strategic
therapy, typically the therapy of substituting a new
action for a habitual one and therefore breaking
a pattern of behaviour. One of the advantages
of following Betty's version is that hunger
often adds a sharpness and clarity to sexual
experience and an orgasm relaxes the
body and floods the brain with enough
endorphins to carry you through the
next twenty minutes until the evening
meal is prepared.

foods to snack on

UK health authorities recommend that
you eat 3-5 pieces of fruit a day to
keep you fit and boost your immune

> "Instead of heading for the
> ice box, steer past it and
> head for the bedroom."

system. This isn't as onerous as it sounds. One piece of fruit can be a grape!

Melon Watermelons contain lycopene which is an anti-oxidant believe to reduce the incidence of cancers. Musk melons act as anti-arthritic agents, cataract preventative, and are also anti cold, depression, glaucoma, migraine, obesity, Parkinson's, ulcer and cancer. Melons are a rich source of beta carotene and vitamin C.

Tangerine and other citrus fruits Small enough to carry, sweet enough to satisfy sweetness cravings, rich in vitamin C – a powerful anti-oxidant, and reported to reduce the risk of cardio-vascular disease and some forms of cancer. An orange a day may keep cancer away.

Apples High in vitamins C and E (anti-oxidants), also high in flavonoids and polyphenols, which reduce oxidisation. Anti-oxidants slow down the aging process.

Grapes The skin of red and purple grapes contain powerful anti-oxidants, having much the same nutritional effect as red wine. Grapes are also an extremely low calorie snack. Grape seed oil can wipe out candida (thrush) from your system.

Bagged mixed seeds Seeds can be purchased from a health food store and placed into a bag the night before work. It is the bigger seeds (pumpkin and sunflower) that make for the most orally satisfying combination but you might add a sprinkling of sesame and an even smaller pinch of linseed.

Pumpkin seeds These are packed with potassium, magnesium, zinc, iron, essential fatty acids believed to help prostate problems, reproductive disorders and help prevent impotence.

Sunflower seeds They satisfy the appetite because of their fat content and prevent fatigue and weariness from sugar lows. Also help balance sodium in our diet thereby protecting us from too much salt in the tissues.

Sesame seeds Believed to relieve rheumatism, constipation, low backache, weak knees and stiff joints. The Turks consider sesame to be the greatest food for building strength.

Linseed A laxative, is the old domestic remedy for colds, coughs and irritation of the urinary organs.

cabbage crunch

Prepare healthy snacks in advance, that can be substituted at key times of the day. That way there is a real food substance to satisfy the "munchies", only now it is healthy snacks that go into your mouth and not sugar highs.

Cabbage crunch can be prepared in advance and bagged for transport to the office. This is a chopped salad that can contain any salad ingredient you like (raw). But it must include either 25 per cent cabbage or 25 per cent of another green vegetable such as raw broccoli or cauliflower, if you truly cannot stand cabbage. If you prepare your salad the night before a working day and store in an air-tight plastic food bag in the refrigerator, it will remain fresh for the rest of the next day. Make enough for both a full meal and a number of small snacks. Incidentally, if you cut salad greens with a plastic knife, the leaves will not suffer from oxidization. Broccoli, cauliflower, Chinese greens, and cabbage are all low in calories, high in insoluble fibre, and make delicious salad crunch. Eating these every day helps prevent cancer of the colon. They are also full of vitamins K and C (to help fight off viruses such as the common cold) and are high in antioxidants (which help delay the ageing process). They contain iron, which assists sexual stamina. In order to maximize your body's absorption of iron, combine such cabbage foods with foods rich in vitamin C, such as red peppers.

herbal and mineral supplements

The 28-Day Plan is not just about getting trim and strong. It's also about bulding up your immunity in such a way as to safeguard your sexual health.

IF YOU AVOID COLDS AND OTHER infections, sleep well regularly, safeguard your prostate, thereby avoiding pain and future incontinence (if you are male), ensure that your menstruation flows easily and without cramps (if you are female), you are going to feel fitter and sexier.

Eat carefully to avoid overloading the digestive system and putting on excess weight. Ensure that you boost your inner health by taking a good multivitamin pill and any of a number of mineral and herbal options (see opposite). Yes, you can get minerals and vitamins from your food. But that assumes you eat all the "right" foods as regularly as clockwork, and that they are virtually all served raw, without the stimulating but neutralizing effects of caffeine. I can't do this. And neither can at least 90 percent of the population I would guess. This is where supplements come in.

Opposite is a list of herbal and mineral supplements that have a specific impact on sexuality or on aspects of health that seriously impinge on sexual experience. Take depression, for example. Anyone who has ever suffered from it will tell you that the first thing to fly out of the window is sexual desire. One of the joys of lifting depression is that your libido usually returns too. Take a look at the following list and see if any of the problems treated seem significant to you. If they do, think about adding a supplement to your diet. If not, leave well enough alone.

herbal supplements

Agnus castus Helps increase sex drive in women, although it has the opposite effect on men. It helps regulate the menstrual cycle and boost some types of female fertility. Don't take with the contraceptive Pill or with HRT.

Black cohosh Helps balance female hormones. Mainly used to relieve menopausal symptoms, it also helps with menstrual cramps, irregular periods, low libido, and PMT. Research shows that standardized black cohosh is at least as effective as HRT; in another study, it did better than diazepam and estrogen HRT in relieving depressive moods and anxiety. Do not take immediately before conception, during pregnancy, or when breastfeeding.

Devil's claw A natural anti-inflammatory that reduces muscle pain, and shoulder and neck pain. Benefits occur about two weeks after starting treatment. Traditionally it has been used to treat the pain of sports injuries, osteoarthritis, and rheumatoid arthritis. Must be taken with food and cannot be used if you suffer from indigestion or peptic ulcers. Avoid during pregnancy and breastfeeding.

Ginger Carries anti-inflammatory and antisickness effects and can be used to counter pregnancy sickness as well as muscle and joint pains and motion sickness.

Ginseng Has been proved to significantly improve sexual performance in men with impotence (see also p.66).

Kelp The supplements are derived from seaweed and are a fantastic nutritional food source, the main ingredient being iodine. It promotes feelings of fullness and also improves the quality of the skin, nails, and hair. Research suggests that a diet high in kelp safeguards your blood pressure and immune function.

St. John's wort An effective antidepressant, it also improves the quality of sleep and helps sufferers of SAD (seasonal affective disorder). In one trial it helped 60 percent of postmenopausal women to regain lost libido. Needs to be taken with food as it can upset digestion. Should not be taken with prescribed antidepressant drugs or with warfarin, oral contraceptives, and a number of other medications or during pregnancy and breastfeeding.

Saw palmetto Helps relieve symptoms of an enlarged prostate gland such as urinary problems. Trials show it to be at least as effective as prescribed drugs for prostate problems without the side-effects such as impotence!

mineral supplements

Boron Improves absorption of calcium and stimulates increased production of estrogen and testosterone. These factors help reduce the risk of osteoporosis and promote bone strength and longevity. Foods containing boron include green vegetables, fruit, and nuts. Osteoporosis is one of the biggest contributing factors to preventing sexual activity.

Calcium Vital to the body for the formation and strength of healthy bones and teeth. Especially important for those with a family history of osteoporosis. Don't forget, men can suffer from it too! Cooking reduces calcium content and high-fiber diets can speed calcium through the body before it can be digested. The best method of absorbing calcium is to drink a pint of low-fat or skimmed milk a day together with a boron supplement. Milk is best drunk at least 20 minutes before a meal since it can interfere with the antioxidant effect of certain foods. If you don't like milk, take a calcium supplement.

Magnesium The other mineral best taken in conjunction with boron and calcium, since it regulates the movement of calcium in and out of cells. You can find magnesium naturally in seafood, seaweed, dark green and leafy vegetables, bananas, and chocolate. Low levels of magnesium have been linked with chronic fatigue and PMT. In supplement form magnesium citrate is most readily absorbed, although magnesium gluconate is less likely to cause an upset stomach.

Selenium Plays a vital role in skin condition and immune function. Low levels can lead to premature wrinkling of the skin, subfertility, age spots, and hair and skin problems. They also seem to increase the risk of miscarriage, and selenium may be useful in fighting cancer. Seriously low levels are responsible for a form of heart failure and muscle and joint degeneration. Brazil nuts are the richest natural source of selenium; other sources are seafood, wholegrains, onions, garlic, broccoli, and cabbage. Selenium works in conjunction with vitamin E.

Zinc Important for sexual maturity, wound healing, and immune function. Oysters are rich in zinc and, since the symptoms of zinc deficiency are delayed puberty, underdeveloped male organs, low sperm count, impaired fertility, and impotence, it is easy to understand oysters' reputation as an aphrodisiac. Each time a man ejaculates he loses around 5mg of zinc, a third of his daily requirement.

passion
killers

Imagine a lover whose breath reeks of alcohol, whose hair and clothes smell of smoke, and who is clearly out of his or her mind on drugs. Not really a seductive picture is it? You wouldn't want to get intimate with someone like this would you?

THERE ARE INNUMERABLE REASONS why tobacco and alcohol ruin your sex life. Here are just a few. Following this are simple suggestions to make the time of withdrawal a little easier.

the dirt on.....smoking

Smoking is just so bad for sex that you wonder why anyone continues with the habit. One US study of men between the ages of 31 and 49 showed a 50 percent increase in the risk of impotence among smokers compared with men who had never smoked. A meta-analysis of studies published since 1980

found that 40 percent of impotent men were current smokers compared with 28 percent of men in the general population. For younger women, smoking and the use of oral contraceptives increases the risk of heart attack, stroke, or other cardiovascular disease tenfold. Menopause occurs up to two years earlier in smokers. Female smokers of more than 10 cigarettes a day run this increased risk.

the dirt on.....booze

As a central nervous system depressant, alcohol numbs nerve endings in the genitalia. That means a drinker needs extra stimulation to produce arousal and orgasm. Alcohol reduces a woman's ability to lubricate, and may cause delayed orgasm. Men experience reduced desire, delayed orgasm, or eventually they can't get an erection at all. Alcohol increases the liver's metabolism (we all know alcohol is bad for the liver); it also causes the liver to turn testosterone into estrogen. With lowered testosterone levels, men experience erectile dysfunction and with prolonged use may grow breasts!

change your diet: break the addiction

You can use a food plan to help you physically overcome problems of addiction. If you eat a diet high in protein when coming off addictive substances, this feeds the brain and can help prevent cravings. The ideal foods to use here are lots of steak or beef, accompanied by tomatoes or salad. Baked potato also works well if you don't want to put on the pounds. Healthy high-protein substances go some way toward satisfying appetite cravings. This diet was originally devised to assist drug addicts and is particularly useful for drug withdrawal. Don't worry if you put on a little weight to start with. Once you are over your withdrawal you can go on a careful eating regimen.

sex plan

When you want to reach for the pack of cigarettes, substitute another form of satisfaction instead. If you are feeling seriously restless, stimulate yourself sexually. Or seduce your lover and use up your energy on lovemaking. The endorphins you experience as a result of orgasm will partially satisfy cravings. You not only tire your body in a healthy fashion, but you also encourage endorphin production. Remember, however, that when you are seducing someone it is not acceptable to pressure a partner into sex. Keep your approach light and playful.

"In going back to your habit you reintroduce to your brain the chemicals that have hooked you before. This is where substitution or strategic sex comes in very handy indeed."

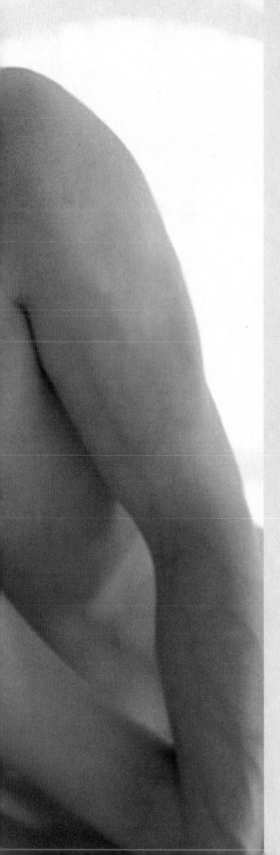

the 28-day plan

THIS IS NOT so much a diet as a healthy eating plan. The idea is to establish a pattern in how and when you eat so that it becomes automatic. Most eating falls into patterns, which means you invariably reach for the chocolate bar at a particular time of day when your energy is low. And your brain gets used to doing this at that hour. But the same can also be true of healthy eating patterns. So we aim to retrain not just your appetite but also your brain. The diet aims to make you fit, assist your digestive processes, and, if you are overweight, streamline your body.

how to use the 28-day plan

Here is some general advice you should read before following the 28-Day Plan. On the next few pages you will also find tips on how to adapt it to your individual needs.

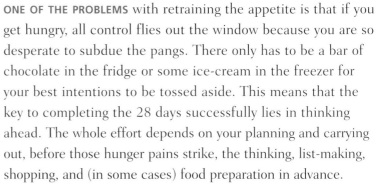

ONE OF THE PROBLEMS with retraining the appetite is that if you get hungry, all control flies out the window because you are so desperate to subdue the pangs. There only has to be a bar of chocolate in the fridge or some ice-cream in the freezer for your best intentions to be tossed aside. This means that the key to completing the 28 days successfully lies in thinking ahead. The whole effort depends on your planning and carrying out, before those hunger pains strike, the thinking, list-making, shopping, and (in some cases) food preparation in advance.

In practical terms this means that the refrigerator needs to be stocked—with the right food. Temptation in whatever form, needs to be quickly removed. But it also means that the healthy alternatives need to be there for you when you rush into the house absolutely starving (see pp.72-73 for some ideas).

plan in advance

To do this you need to browse through the Plan in advance, perhaps a week at a time, and plan to go shopping on the weekend preceding each week. If you have a day with more time than others, this might be the occasion on which to cook the dishes that can be prepared in advance and put them in the freezer. If you know you are always hungry midafternoon, equip yourself with bags full of chopped fresh vegetables, seeds, and rice crackers. These are far healthier alternatives to cakes, cookies, and candy.

remove pesticide

Since there are now proven to be high levels of pesticide used on some fruit and vegetables, it is a good idea to scrub all veg and fruit before using. And if you are still worried, scrubbing a hard fruit, such as an apple, with vinegar is the most likely means of thoroughly cleaning the skin. Always buy organic if you've got the option of doing so.

sleep and food

If you know that you are always starving just before you go to bed at night, bear in mind that this is almost certainly your body telling you that its energy resources are depleted, and it has overdrawn on food absorption. Sleep is the cure here, not food, but getting to sleep when your stomach feels empty is not so easy. The trick is to fool your stomach into thinking it is full. A large glass of water immediately before bedtime can do this.

sleep and sex

So too can the calming effects of good, loving sex. Just being held by the one you love is calming and the actual release of physical tension through orgasm fills the body with endorphins that relax you, reassure you, and let you fall asleep.

I've described some specific sexual activities in the Plan that fit in with the kind of digestion of the food in the menus. But… and it's a big but, I don't believe in prescribed sex. These are merely suggestions and if you have other ideas, that's wonderful. Go for them! The only things I would remind you are that it is easy to get stuck in a pattern of regular lovemaking because it works well. This is fine for the early years but it leads to boredom. If you have gotten into the habit of having a lot less sex than you would really like (and just about every sex survey reveals that 50 percent of the respondents are unsatisfied with what goes on in their sexual relationship), following my suggestions is a useful method of getting back in touch!

the basic
pattern

If you can't be bothered to go through each day of the Plan in detail, you can instead work from the absolute basics. See right for the bare bones of the plan. If you only stick to these principles for a few weeks you will lose weight.

the bare bones

The 28-Day Plan is made up of four week-long sections, each of which includes the following pattern.

Day 1 Vegetables, no potato, fruit

Day 2 Vegetables, potato, no fruit

Day 3 Vegetables, no potato, fruit

Day 4 Vegetables, no potato, fruit (bananas only)

Day 5 Meat, vegetables (tomatoes), no potato, no fruit, extra water

Day 6 Oily fish, vegetables, no potato, fruit

Day 7 Meat, vegetables, no potato, fruit, extra water

Always eat one portion of fruit at breakfast and a good multivitamin supplement. If you want to maintain your diet, make the addition of up to two slices of bread a day, or more potatoes. On Days 6 and 7 you can have either a glass of red wine or 100g of plain chocolate.

the key elements

There may be days when you are unable to follow the Plan, or when you simply want a day off. If this is the case, make sure that you eat food that has the following qualities:

- Virtually no fat (only tiny amounts of virgin olive oil)
- No sugar
- Low salt
- Cut out wheat (in any form) while losing weight
- No diary products except regular skimmed milk
- Balanced protein and carbohydrate
- Occasional potassium intake
- Extremely high fiber
- As much raw food as possible.

safe sex

Protect yourself from sexually transmitted diseases by taking note of the following guidelines:

Wait Leave full sexual intercourse until you are older. Young women's interior sex organs may still be immature and as a result, they can catch sexual illnesses such as herpes and warts more easily. These infections can have long-term consequences, since there may be a link between early infection and the development of cervical cancer.

Use a condom This protects against many sexual infections, including those above, plus condoms are also a major barrier against HIV infection.

Just say no If you think there may be any health risk, don't be afraid of saying no.

Learn how to put on a condom correctly The best method is to squeeze the tip between finger and thumb and then roll the condom down the erect penis. Never unroll the condom first and then try to put it on.

Always carry a condom This also applies to young women. Older men and women who have returned to a life of dating should carry condoms too.

Trying it on Don't be afraid to turn condom-fitting into a game; for example, try putting one on your partner with your mouth only!

Retrain your mind Associate the act and scent of putting on a condom with being erotic. It can be an exciting high point.

83

how much food does a healthy body need?

Being overweight can be a major downer on your sex life. But how many calories do you really need if you want to lose weight but remain healthy and energetic?

IN THE WEST one in five people (at least) is now seriously obese. This doesn't mean just fat; it means massive. And contrary to the idea that quite a lot of roundness is sexy (which it is), really massive individuals don't enjoy good sex because they cannot physically move. Far more important, though, is the considerable strain put on the heart by the sheer effort of carrying what amounts to an extra person around with them all day long. Overweight is a major health hazard as well as a sex-life killer.

count your calories

So I make no excuses for offering a food plan, which allows you to lose weight if that's what you chose. The average man needs 2,500 calories a day to maintain weight and 1,500 to lose some. The average woman needs 1,900 calories to maintain weight and 1,200 to lose some. These figures are only a guide because different genetic inheritance, height, and age all play a part in what you individually need.

when plump is good!

It's also clear that there are some phases of life where it's natural to be plump. Young teenagers are often naturally plump and so are middle-aged women, women of that uncertain age whose metabolism has started to slow down. Teenagers usually grow out of their plumpness (literally) during their final growth spurt, but it doesn't hurt should they get a lot more physical exercise than they may have been used to. Dieting is not recommended for young teenagers, but healthy eating is.

calorific counting

Here are a few facts you might like to know when deciding on your diet. For every gram of fat in any type of food you gain nine calories. For every gram of protein (as in meat) or carbohydrate (as in potato or sugar) you gain four calories. No prizes for guessing which to cut out. Lots of salt causes the tissues to retain fluid and raises blood pressure, which ups the likelihood of a stroke. But we all need some salt, so it is a mistake to cut it out completely. Ideally we need around 3g of salt a day, so we should read the labels on processed food carefully, since the salt content is often high. The only thing we cannot get enough of is fiber. So if you want to seriously pig out, go for vegetables, salad, legumes, fruit, and high-fiber cereals such as muesli.

middle-aged spread

Middle-aged women DO need to take action. They don't need as much food as they did when younger, but it is extremely difficult to retrain the brain, which has had years of a regular food pattern. Hence the value of the 28-Day Plan, which attempts precisely that. Older people too may have developed poor digestion through years of abusing their innocent stomachs. Finding out your specific food tolerances does not just make you feel better, but can also make you thinner. Regular exercise is vital, however old you are!

alcohol and impotence

Those who live within a beer or alcohol culture, meeting every night at the bar with the guys, competing to drink, also develop some very strange body shapes—the most notable for men being breasts and a huge belly. In addition, men lose flexibility of movement, lower their sperm count, and increase the likelihood of becoming impotent. If you honestly have the strength of mind to ration your alcohol successfully, then now is the time to do so (see p.77 for some advice on how to do it).

85

how much sex does a healthy body need?

Sex is very definitely something that you need the right feelings and emotions for. It is not something that you can deliberately control because if you do not possess the desire or love, you cannot automatically make your body turn on.

ASKING HOW MUCH SEX you need is a bit like asking how much food you need. There is no genuine average of sexual intercourse, nor should we be driven by what we think we ought to be doing.

There has been relatively little serious research done on how good or bad for the body sex can be. We do know that gentle sex for men and women who are heart patients is good for them, whereas highly stressed sex can be bad for the same group. Some studies have shown that regular sex does not necessarily keep you any healthier. However, since it's also true to say that if you feel under the weather or actually disabled sex tends to fly out of the window anyway, these findings probably don't mean much.

we are what we believe

A lot of how we function sexually is down to how we believe we ought to. At the moment there seems to be an epidemic of celibacy among young couples in their late 20s and early 30s. And it's no accident that this happens at a time of life most consumed by other demands. Women as well as men are working these days and are just plain exhausted. Bringing up children in an urban environment is hard and so too is the uncertainty of employment. Stress is a common cause for diminishing sexual activity. Perhaps the fact that it is happening to all our friends makes it all right for us to lessen our loving.

it gets better when you are older

The good news is that this can all improve. Many older couples now figure they are having a better sex life than the younger ones, probably because they have more time and

just think!

A diary (see opposite) is a good opportunity to think about sex. But so too is a long walk. Many people find that musing on a problem during exercise, they reach a solution toward the end. What might you consider during this process? Your relationship is one good choice. How do you feel about it? Are there weaknesses that could be strengthened? Is there an issue that is preventing real intimacy and you know needs to be tackled? Here is also an opportunity to work out how to have a necessary confrontation.

therefore feel more relaxed. Modern medication means that men don't have to fear impotence as they did in the past and the right hormone treatment can help retain a woman's interest.

we may not live forever but we can give it a darn good try

In the past we believed that we would be unable to move around much when older, that the sex drive would die, that menopause cut off a woman's physical, and to some extent emotional, life. As a result, the beliefs tended to come true. Today we do think we are going to last longer. Today's 60 year olds have got different expectations from the previous generation's. Many people find love or remarry after the age of 60 and business is constantly targeting the older consumer. Sixty years ago women were old at 50—literally gray-haired, overweight, and sedentary. Today, at the age of 50 we are hardly hitting middle age.

It's fair to say that 18-23 year olds are likely to have a lot of sex; that it will diminish a bit for the 24-29 year olds; that for the 30-49 year olds it will diminish a lot. After that the figures creep up again until the 70s. Can we still look forward to sex in old age? We now know that provided you keep using the body, literally exercising your muscle groups, you can stay fit into extreme old age. As long as you do not suffer from a debilitating illness, a good sex life can last forever—this is not a fairy tale but the truth.

losing weight is the key

So the likelihood is that if we look after our bodies, our sex life will continue for a long time. If you reduce weight, your joints will have to carry less and last longer; your lungs won't get worn out puffing all that extra oxygen around the body and putting a strain on your heart. Plus, if you get regular, gentle exercise, you will continue to be able to use your muscles in all kinds of pleasing ways. So if sex is one of your priorities now, think about making it a priority for when you are aged 70!

keeping a sex diary

It's good to keep a record of how you are feeling generally; whether you're full of energy or not. Also record how you are feeling sexually. Do you long for sex, enjoy it when it comes, and feel constant desire? Does sexual desire sharpen when you are hungry? Or do you find it is only occasional, and at very specific times of the month? If you compare corresponding days in your 28-day month, you will see some patterns begin to emerge. Women of course really need a comparison of their menstrual months, so it might be a good idea to keep a menstruation diary. It is also worth noting down which position gives you the most or least pleasure and if there is any connection between weight loss and sexual activity. You might also note down the quality of your orgasms and whether they were enjoyed with your partner or on your own.

sleep, hormones, and loving

Exhaustion is a sex killer. So is tension. If you are subject to a particularly tense way of life, get regular physical exercise, on the grounds that it dissipates much of the tension.

WE ALL KNOW ABOUT the endorphins that course around the body after exercise—and that includes sexual exercise. Among other things, endorphins relax us and help us sleep. So to get your beauty sleep, get in the exercise too.

soft exercise

It's no longer thought necessary to do strenuous exercise. One of the problems with tough aerobics and jogging is that you can pull muscles and, more worryingly, permanently damage your cartilage and joints. The good news is that Pilates exercises, properly done, can keep you strong, offer mild exercise, and give you an endorphin rush. So too can brisk walking, swimming, and gardening.

hormones and sleep

Sleep is literally a beauty treatment. It heals wounds, allows bone and muscle to recuperate, dissipates fluid (from the face), and allows the skin to look glowing and young. Hormones are another important area. We are all born with certain built-in levels of hormones and our bodies use them from day one of our lives. If you are male you are largely motivated by the hormone testosterone, which gives strength, energy, and sex drive. These levels fall very gradually from the mid-20s onward and it is normal for most men around the 50s and 60s to experience a lessened sensitivity of the skin, lessened sexual response, and lower sexual desire. Women too are driven by hormones, partly in fluctuating cycles. Every menstrual month the levels of estrogen, progesterone and, to a much lesser degree, testosterone go through regular changes. During menopause (around the age of 50) these levels rapidly and naturally decrease, leaving a much decreased sex drive and physical sensitivity.

hormone supplements

The wonders of today's medicine mean that men can now take testosterone supplements and Viagra-type medication to ensure that their energy and ability to experience erection are sustained. Women, too, can benefit from hormone boost, as they go through menopause, to sustain their energy and youthfulness. This includes testosterone supplements to maintain sex drive and sensation. The women who should not opt for hormone replacement are those with a history of breast cancer in their family. There is now available a range of natural substances that help ease menopause and prolong sexual life (see pp.74-75), but you will also find that one of the benefits of exercising is that this too can prolong hormone activity.

keep fit basics

Ideally, even if you lead the most sedentary life, you should:
• Every two and a half hours lie down with your shoulders propped slightly up and your knees bent, for 20 minutes. This takes normal, every-day pressure off your spine.
• Get in one good walk, preferably at a time of day when you are not exhausted. If you work in an office, the lunch hour is the obvious time for this.
• Once a week, enjoy a special activity such as Pilates, or swimming, or even something more rigorous like squash or tennis.

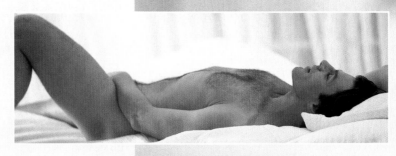

ALL GOOD DIETS, be they for losing or for putting on weight, start with detoxifying the body. In the 28-Day Plan, we depend strongly on green vegetables, in particular cabbage, to help us clear the digestive system. Cabbage fills you up, but also seems to act as a diuretic. If you cannot eat cabbage, substitute other members of the brassica family instead, such as sprouts, kale, broccoli, or cauliflower. Remember that the Plan is intended to be comfortable on your digestion, so if any food makes you feel bloated, leave it out.

In addition to the food in the daily menu, eat a good vitamin and mineral supplement. Take your supplement only after food and preferably with a glass of skimmed milk. (see pp.74-75 for advice on taking supplements.)

eat me

Breakfast	One large piece of fruit such as orange, sweet grapefruit, or half a melon. NO bananas.
Lunch	Vegetable soup (see p.146 for recipe): include fresh carrots, mushrooms, chopped cabbage, (green or white), one finely diced medium potato. No bread.
Dinner	Grilled mushrooms and tomatoes (as many as you feel you can eat) accompanied by a quarter of cooked cabbage. (If you find you want more cabbage to fill up on, here is where you get to know what amounts suit you.) Dessert consists of fresh raspberries but with no cream or sugar.
Sex snack	Raw celery. It's anti-inflammatory, great if you're moving your arms and legs around a lot.

bedtime tip If you're still hungry at bedtime, drink a glass of water to fill you up.

please yourself

Many people feel surprisingly full after the first day. So you may not feel up to acrobatic activity with your partner. Declare this a For Yourself night. If you sleep on your own you will have no difficulty here. If you share a bedroom with your partner, negotiate some time for yourself or spend longer than usual in the bathroom.

   Pamper your body in a warm bath full of sweet-smelling oils and give yourself a self-massage in a warm room. Let the self-massage culminate in climax. Try self-stimulation from a variety of positions including on all fours and on your stomach. Exercise several different areas of the body before allowing yourself to experience orgasm and that wonderful slide into restfulness.

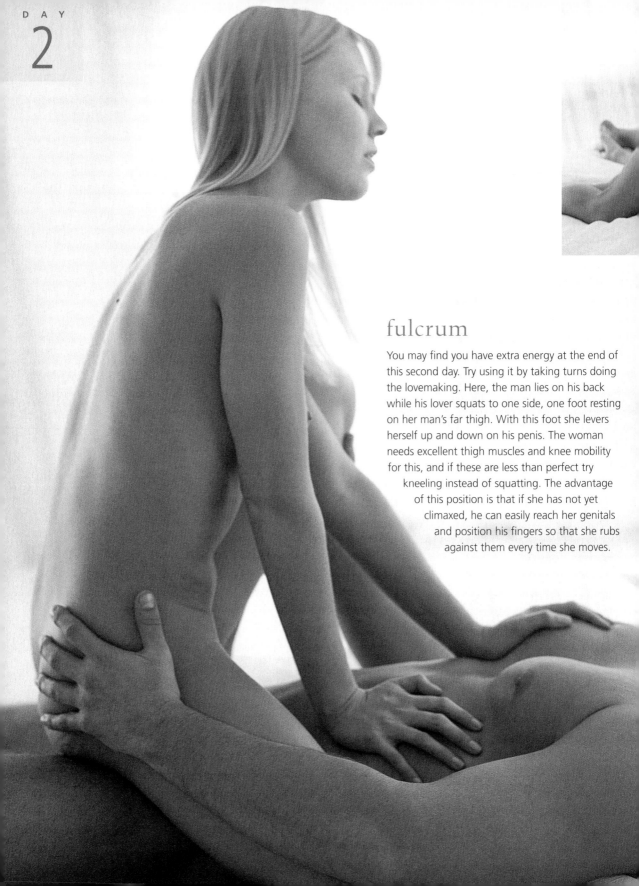

fulcrum

You may find you have extra energy at the end of this second day. Try using it by taking turns doing the lovemaking. Here, the man lies on his back while his lover squats to one side, one foot resting on her man's far thigh. With this foot she levers herself up and down on his penis. The woman needs excellent thigh muscles and knee mobility for this, and if these are less than perfect try kneeling instead of squatting. The advantage of this position is that if she has not yet climaxed, he can easily reach her genitals and position his fingers so that she rubs against them every time she moves.

grating the nutmeg

In this man-on-top position called Grating the Nutmeg, the woman lies on her back with the man on top in missionary style. But instead of thrusting in and out, the man presses his pelvis close to hers and moves from side to side and around and around so that her clitoris is being massaged, in much the same way as you might rub a nutmeg on a grater. This is likely to bring her to orgasm, or very close to it.

THE GOAL OF THIS BOOK is to encourage fitness through sexuality and great sex through fitness. It's a seesaw notion where one benefits the other. As you begin to feel better (and possibly slimmer), you will find that your body craves more touch and responds to it with greater eagerness. So spend a lot more time on caressing. As your body detoxifies through cutting out most (but not all) fats, sugars, wheat, and dairy products, you'll find you enjoy lots more energy. Use it to give your adored partner an amazing full-body treat.

Spend time caressing your partner's body before approaching anywhere near the genital area. They will be literally on fire with sensuality all over their body before any specifically sexual moves are made. As a result, the eventual climaxes that you experience will be unusually long, strong, and powerful.

eat me

Breakfast	A large piece of fruit such as a big apple or a small bunch of grapes.
Lunch	Fresh, raw, or even canned vegetables. Try to include raw shredded cabbage and other leafy, green veg. Stay away from beans, peas, and corn.
Supper	Wok-fried red cabbage with grated apple, a drop of balsamic vinegar, and sunflower seeds cooked in extra virgin olive oil. Season with a little salt. Serve with a large baked potato and eat until you feel full. Do not eat any more fruit today. Reserve some of the cabbage mixture for tomorrow. It keeps well in a covered dish and is delicious cold.
Sex snack	A box of fresh vegetables cut into sticks or florets—carrot, celery, red pepper, and raw cauliflower.

drinks Drink only tea, black coffee, or water today—do not drink any fruit juice.

CABBAGE CASSEROLE is the vital ingredient of Day Three (for recipe, see p.146). Make it at the beginning of the day or the night before so that you can eat right away when you come home in the evening. Planning is crucial if you want to stop yourself snacking from snacking on sweets and cookies. You can make a larger quantity and keep the extra in the refrigerator; or store it in a thermos flask, if you want to eat while on the run.

If you have not cheated during these first three days you will have lost around five pounds. You won't lose weight in a hurry on the Sex Diet—the food consumption together with the sexercise means that any weight loss is gradual. For the first weeks you cut all wheat out of the diet completely. Drinks are the usual coffee or tea (with no sugar) or water.

eat me

Breakfast	One large portion of fruit. A peach, half a melon, or a large apple, or three or four canned prunes.
Lunch	Eat a varied salad that includes chopped cabbage, grated carrot, baby tomatoes, lots of different salad greens, and sunflower seeds. If you are female and over 40, add a sprinkling of linseeds.
Dinner	Eat as much of the cabbage casserole as you can eat. Any kind of fruit is fine for dessert. If you are still hungry, eat more of the salad above. You are allowed a small amount of salad dressing here but check the brands—some are packed with calories, others are not. Go for the least calorific, but don't settle for anything that tastes unpleasant.
Sex snack	If you want something to munch on, try rice crackers, which are seriously low in calories.

1 Begin in the basic lovemaking position, with one partner on top. The partner underneath should lie with both legs between those of his partner.

2 The partner on top lifts first the left leg and then the right leg over her partner's right leg, without letting the penis slip from the vagina.

3 Supporting herself on her arms, the partner on top moves both legs farther around, until her body is at a right angle to that of her partner below.

the turning position

This fun position first appeared in the *Kama Sutra* around the 4th century AD. The partner on top (who can be either the man or the woman) turns in a circle of 180 degrees without once letting the penis slip from the vagina. In order to achieve the turn, the partner on top (here, the woman) needs to lean on her arms, which means using the strength she has built up there. At the same time, with great care, she lifts her legs around in a semicircle, one after the other. To do this, without giving your partner an unwelcome blow to the face, you need to be capable of raising your legs and holding them in a raised position for as long as it takes. (See pp.22-23 for Pilates leg and buttock exercises that will help with balance and strengthening the relevant muscles.)

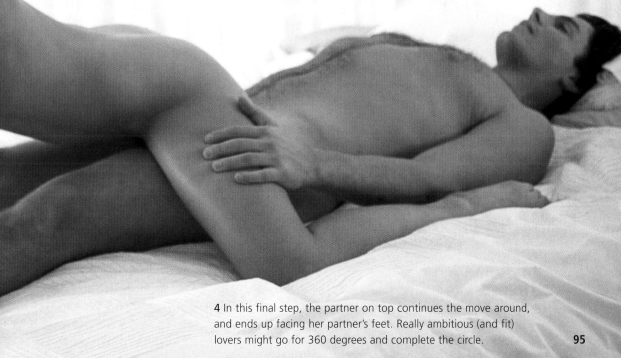

4 In this final step, the partner on top continues the move around, and ends up facing her partner's feet. Really ambitious (and fit) lovers might go for 360 degrees and complete the circle.

ONE OF THE DIFFICULTIES WITH DIETS is that any food regimen where you eat only selected foods means that your body will start to lack certain important vitamins and minerals. This is why I recommend a daily intake of supplements to safeguard your health and also why I nominate certain days on which you eat specific food substances to balance your digestive process.

The banana recommended here is to be eaten, not used for sexual purposes—sorry to disappoint you! On Day Four you eat as many bananas and drink as many glasses of skimmed milk as you can. Bananas are high in calories and carbohydrates and so is milk, but on this particular day your body will need the potassium, carbohydrates, and calcium to lessen your craving for sugar.

eat me

Breakfast	Bananas and skimmed milk—as much as you can eat and drink.
Lunch	The usual varied salad, complete with seeds and shredded cabbage and a small amount of salad dressing. Dessert can be bananas and milk.
Dinner	White Night. Wokked white cabbage, fried in a tiny amount of virgin pressed olive oil, with garlic seeds to taste, chopped leek and mushrooms, plus a tiny amount of salt. Just before serving stir in a sprinkling of caraway seed. Serve with plain, heated cannellini beans. For dessert, bananas sprinkled with lemon juice and a small amount of brown sugar. Pop in the microwave for one minute on medium.
Sex snack	No surprise—it's those curvy yellow fruits.

diet tip Write down every single food you put in your mouth. This can be surprisingly helpful in making you pause and rethink what you eat.

the encircling position

This posture is only really possible if you are flexible, so enter into it carefully. Such is the pressure of the man up against the woman's crossed ankles that her knee joints are likely to be pushed outward and her pelvis opened wide as he thrusts forward. If the encircling position begins to HURT, ask your partner to withdraw. And practice the Rollup (see p.35) and the *Plié* (see p.29) so that your back and your knees become more limber.

While lying on her back, the woman raises her feet off the bed a little and crosses her calves so that her legs form a diamond shape. Then the man lies over her and enters her, thrusting up against her crossed ankles.

a sensual massage

After doing without it for a week, it is surprising how heavily a large portion of meat sits on your stomach. Meat takes much longer to pass through the digestive system than vegetables. Today is not a day for energetic intercourse but rather for taking things easy. A sensual massage (avoiding the abdomen) satisfies the skin's need for touch, and offers exercise to the person giving it.

Wait until an hour after the meal. A good massage is done in a warm room, with warm hands and warmed (not boiling) massage oil.

Circling

The most useful stroke for sensual massage is the circling stroke. With both palms flat, circle your hands away from the spine and out toward the side of the body. You can travel up and down the body with circling. Perform every stroke as if in slow motion. The slower the massage, the sexier it is. Once you have rubbed the oil in, never take both hands completely off the skin.

The Glide A final spectacular stroke is the glide. Here you position yourself astride your partner's thighs, place your palms flat on the underside of the buttocks, and lean on your hands. Let the weight of your body push your hands up over the buttocks and along the back until they end at the shoulders, where you pull them around to the sides and down the arms. It feels absolutely wonderful.

IT WON'T HAVE ESCAPED YOUR NOTICE that for the past four days you have been eating mostly vegetables and fruit. This has been on the grounds that vegetables and fruit are much easier to digest than meat and because the fiber in vegetables helps cleanse you from the inside. But it is not good for us to be without protein altogether.

There's a school of thought that believes the best diet for us is the caveman's, because it is the diet that man evolved with. Cavemen ate mainly fresh shoots, roots, and fruit. Every few days they would catch fish and every month or so there would be a hunt when a large animal would be eaten. The 28-Day Plan follows this natural regimen and it is on Day Five that we eat a portion of lean beef. Beef is the meat of choice because it consists of densely packed protein and not too much fat.

eat me

Breakfast	Make yourself a huge smoothie. Purée together fruits such as mango, papaya, orange, strawberries, and any fruit you like, except banana. This sets your digestive processes up for the first meat you are about to eat, in the week. Do NOT add sugar.
Lunch	Choice of either shredded cabbage salad or, if you prefer a change, some saved (or newly made) vegetable casserole. As much of this as you can eat. No fruit.
Dinner	Beef and tomatoes. Eat up to 20 oz of beef and a can of tomatoes, or as many as six fresh tomatoes. Drink up to six glasses of water today to wash away the uric acid. No more fruit.
Sex snack	Blanch some asparagus stalks or tips, so that they are cooked but not mushy. These act as a diuretic, expelling excess fluid from your body.

TODAY IS OILY FISH DAY. The 28-Day Plan is a fat-burning diet, but it is fat-burning in moderation. The secret, in the first week, is that you burn more calories than you take in. But you do need some fat in the diet for good health, plus nutritionists tell us we ought to eat regular portions of oily fish. Fish oils don't just stave off coughs and colds, but also safeguard against rheumatism and types of arthritis.

Fish is also supposed to be good for the brain and our exercises today aim to increase sexual concentration. So today we eat oily fish, such as salmon or mackerel. We'll still gain valuable protein as a result, but we'll also get those valuable fish oils. If you absolutely hate fish, eat a second portion of beef today but remember to supplement your diet with fish-oil capsules.

eat me

Breakfast	A half or even a whole sweet grapefruit, but with no additional sugar.
Lunch	Belgian endive (chicory), sweet orange salad, and cannellini beans with sunflower seeds to provide a crunchy sensation.
Dinner	Salmon or mackerel microwaved. This cooking process conserves the fish's natural juices, but it does need a lid or cover (nonmetallic) to prevent spattering. Serve with as many leafy green vegetables as you want, especially broccoli. Dessert is sliced strawberries mixed with raspberries and a light sprinkling of brown sugar.
Sex snack	Prepare in advance small bags of mixed seeds, such as pumpkin and sunflower, to dip into at moments of hunger.

kama's wheel

This positions uses sex as a kind of meditation on the theory that it can bring us to a high level of awareness, a sharpness of appetite, and an increased sense of well-being. The object of the exercise is not to build erotic feeling or to achieve orgasm. It is rather to obtain a balance of mind that feels clear, calm, and happy.

The man sits with his legs outstretched and parted, and his partner lowers herself on to his penis, extending her legs over his. He then puts his arms on each side of her body, keeping them straight. In this way he completes the spokelike pattern of limbs that gives the position its name. The couple then rocks gently, offering just enough sensation to sustain erection and to feel in mental harmony.

"Never, ever serve oysters in a month that has no pay check in it."

P. J. O'Rourke

IF YOU HAVE NOT CHEATED, you should have lost around 5 or 7 lbs by the end of your first week. You will have cleared your system of any food matter that was clogging up your digestion and you will have avoided all wheat products and most dairy products. This means your body is now thoroughly detoxed. If you find you are relying heavily on cups of tea and coffee to stave off hunger pangs, you might experiment during the second week by substituting some of the herbal teas that are now easily available. Some tea and a little coffee *is good for you.*

If you feel satisfied with your progress so far you can reward yourself at the evening meal with either one glass of red wine or a small amount of chocolate. Both contain substances that are valuable for good health. Try to make the chocolate as plain and as good quality as you can. But limit yourself to 3½ oz (100g).

eat me

Breakfast	Fresh fruit salad.
Lunch	Freshly cooked new potatoes, tossed in olive oil and chopped basil, accompanied by a plate of delicious shredded cabbage, carrot, and apple, tossed in lemon juice. As much as you can eat.
Dinner	Your second beef day. Eat a smaller portion of steak for this meal, accompanied by grilled tomatoes and plain boiled cabbage, served with a (very) small dab of olive-oil-based margarine. Dessert may be either fresh fruit or a small portion of canned fruit provided it is canned in juice and NOT syrup.
Sex snack	Apple fingers: apple portions with peel left on, sprinkled with lemon juice to prevent browning.

food tip Drink at least six glasses of water today to wash away uric acid from the body.

the scissors

This position is great for men and women wanting to get as much sensation out of intercourse as possible. It has such potential for feeling good: it's fitting, therefore, that this should be the reward for sticking with the first week of the 28-Day Plan.

The woman lies on her back on the ground with her legs straight out in front of her. The man penetrates her from above with his legs also stretched out as straight as possible. Once he is inside her she squeezes her thighs together so that he is effectively penetrating her thighs as well as her vagina. This doubles the sensual sensation he receives and it focuses sensitivity for her. The longer sense of pulling as he moves away from her can be extremely erotic.

use your sexual energy

One of the advantages of not being overfull
is that you feel more energetic. Today might,
therefore, be a good day for you to use your
body actively to pleasure each other. Start with
a woman-on-top position, described in the
Kama Sutra as A Pair of Tongs.

   With her legs bent at the knees, the woman
sits astride and facing the man, who lies flat on
his back. She draws his penis inside her and,
repeatedly squeezing it with the muscles
of her vagina, eventually moves on to very
slowly rising and falling above him, while
still squeezing internally. This sounds as if
it is mild exercise but, in fact, it takes
quite precise muscle control in the
thighs and buttocks. Tomorrow,
it's the man's turn to be active.

"Other things are just food. But chocolate is chocolate."

Patrick Skene Catling

ON THE SECOND WEEK you begin to perceive the pattern that your eating now assumes. Today it returns to a similar pattern to that of Day One.

The diet cuts out most fats, restricts you to vegetables for four of the seven days, and, while you are trying to lose weight, orders how you eat those vegetables (you can't always eat potatoes as well as green vegetables, only occasionally). You can't always eat fruit as a snack or a dessert, because it contains fructose, a natural sugar. You'll also notice that you cut out wheat and dairy products, except milk. Your digestion should feel more comfortable and the high fiber in the vegetables and fruit should mean that waste expulsion works well.

eat me

Breakfast	One large piece of fruit (not bananas). Citrus fruit is good because it fills you up and provides fiber. Don't be afraid to swallow a proportion of the pith that covers the citrus fruit, it's good for your insides.
Lunch	A huge salad with an assortment of salad leaves, chopped red cabbage, a chopped apple, washed, canned cannellini beans, and a sprinkling of sunflower seeds. Add a little chopped red pepper to aid digestion. No seasoning and no bread.
Dinner	Gently cook a large bunch of asparagus in lightly salted water and serve with a little olive-oil-based margarine plus thin green beans and as much plain cooked cabbage as you can eat. Dessert consists of chopped fresh strawberries, preferably eaten without sugar. If you crave sweetening, sprinkle with a sugar-substitute powder. If you have eaten enough cabbage you shouldn't feel hungry after this.
Sex snack	If you still feel hungry on your all-veg and no protein day try a thin scraping of yeast extract on a rice cracker.

food tip You can substitute broccoli or cauliflower for the cabbage if you prefer.

TODAY'S MENU FOLLOWS the pattern of Day Two. It is a day of vegetables, some carbohydrate, but no fruit. On the second week we are still aiming at slow weight loss and this day is one of the main weight loss occasions. If you are not following this diet for weight loss but want to maintain your weight while eating healthily, you may add fruit but

not otherwise. Don't forget to take your mineral and vitamin supplements to fill you with healthy energy!

If you feel hungry between meals have a glass of water to drink, but don't drink more than five cups of liquid during the day. Like anything else, too much water can bloat you, so make a note of your fluid intake.

eat me

Breakfast	A large bowl of plain cornflakes with a lot of skimmed milk. No sugar or fruit.
Lunch	A crunchy, mixed salad
Dinner	White Night, wokked cabbage (see p.96)
Sex snack	Prepare sticks of celery, cucumber, and carrot and keep in an air-tight container so that you can dip in when you like.

drinks Drink only tea, black coffee, or water today—do not drink any fruit juices.

pressing her body

Today it is the man's turn to be sexually active and a man-on-top position called Pressing Her Body facilitates this. Pressing Her Body consists of the woman lying on her back with the man lying stretched along her body, face-to-face. Most of the front of his body touches most of the front of her body! Her legs are slightly open and his legs stretch out between them. Thrusting for him depends on a flexible back and good thigh and buttock control, while all movement pivots on his knees. He will also need strong forearms to lift his upper body slightly, in order not to crush his partner with his weight.

AS WITH DAY THREE, this is another special weight-loss day. You will need generous helpings of the Cabbage Casserole recipe (see p.146) and it may be easier to prepare it the night before so that it is readily available at mealtimes.

The casserole will be your main food source today. As this is the second week of the Plan, experiment with the recipe by adding herbs and spices to make it as tasty for your individual needs as possible. You may like to add tomatoes or other vegetables, but remember that corn, peas, and parsnips are not recommended, since they are laden with natural sugars. If you want to flavor with stock cubes, check the fat content. Avoid chicken cubes, since they are often high in fat.

"Never eat more than you can lift."

Miss Piggy

eat me

Breakfast	Half a large, sweet melon or several slices of watermelon. Don't worry if you swallow the seeds—they will act as roughage and are nutritious.
Lunch	This consists of as much of the cabbage casserole as you can eat (see p.146 for recipe). Prepare in advance. Do not supplement with bread or potato or pasta. Don't forget pasta is made with wheat flour and for this second week wheat is still off the menu. If you are still hungry, fill up on more of the casserole.
Dinner	As this is a special weight-loss day, dinner is more cabbage casserole and the same rule (as lunchtime) applies. Don't add potatoes, bread, or pasta. Instead, fill up on second helpings of the casserole. Eat fruit for dessert. You might like the second half of the melon or a fresh fruit salad, but without added sugar or cream.
Sex snack	Bag up handfuls of seeds and fill up on these when that snacky feeling strikes.

soothing the savage breast

Today and tomorrow you will use the Betty Dodson method of substituting one pleasurable activity for another. Deflect your sugar or fat cravings by giving your body a massive amount of tactile attention.

Today the woman will massage the man, using firm, strong massage strokes (see pp.24-25 for suggestions) and will spend at least half an hour covering his entire body, front and back. At the end of the full body massage she will graduate to massaging his genitals, ending either with him reaching climax or, if you don't like doing this via mutual masturbation, going on to intercourse. Genital massage is done much like any other massage, in that it experiments with different strokes and pressures. The genitals need to be slippery, so don't be afraid of using massage oil or special lubricants.

TODAY IS THE LAST of the vegetable-only days for Week Two. As with Day Four of the previous week, you are allowed as many bananas and as much skimmed milk as you can eat and drink. This goes a long way toward filling up any corners left empty with hunger and satisfies your weekly requirements for potassium and calcium.

You should be taking supplements EVERY day while on the 28-Day Plan, and my occasional mentions are simply reminders. Given the high vitamin and mineral content of vegetables, many of which you will eat raw while on the Plan, you should be fine, but the 28-Day Plan leaves nothing to chance!

eat me

Breakfast	Bananas with skimmed milk. Today you can take your vitamins and minerals either with water or with skimmed milk.
Lunch	A huge raw salad of salad leaves, thinly chopped red cabbage, grated fresh celeriac (celery root) and carrot, and—if you are not allergic—a sprinkling of coarsely chopped walnuts and low-calorie dressing.
Dinner	Cabbage moussaka (see p.146 for recipe). This nutrititious vegetable dish only takes about 15 minutes to prepare (including precooking the vegetables) and a further 30 minutes to bake in the oven. The casserole can be followed by a dessert of more bananas.
Sex snack	Melon—tons of it. And leave it out of the refrigerator so that it ripens and becomes sweet.

tip The best salad dressing is good olive oil and balsamic vinegar, with a little seasoning.

feeding her skin

On the same principles as yesterday, today is a touching occasion. Begin by coating both your bodies with massage oil and then literally roll around each other so that your body massages your partner's body with your torso alone. Once you have covered as much skin as is humanly possible with this unconventional massage method, it is his turn to give good strokes. Cover her body, back and front, with firm but gentle massage touch (see pp.24-25 for details), and don't forget to include her limbs, hands, and feet. Finish by giving a genital massage consisting of different strokes and pressures applied in a particularly rhythmic routine. She may climax this way, or the pair of you may prefer to finish with intercourse.

THIS IS THE DAY when, as your caveman ancestors might have done, you supplement your mainly vegetable diet with some protein. Fortunately, you don't have to go out and shoot the animal with your bow and arrow, but I suspect you'll enjoy your large portion of lean red beef just as much as your clan fathers and mothers! Don't forget: the body takes longer to digest meat than vegetables. This means that it's a good idea to eat this evening's meal earlier than usual in order to give your stomach acids some extra time to break down the meat protein before it is time to sleep.

eat me

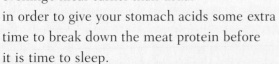

Breakfast	Blend together any of the following: mango, peach, apricot, papaya, strawberry, raspberry, blackberry, and skimmed milk. Add half a banana to thicken and a little lemon juice for taste. But NO sugar.
Lunch	Choice of fresh, shredded raw salad or, if you prefer, a portion of cabbage moussaka, prepared the previous evening (see p.147 for recipe). You might keep the leftover casserole to use as a vegetable to accompany this evening's meat course.
Dinner	Beef and tomatoes. You may eat up to 20 ounces of beef and a can of tomatoes or as many as six fresh tomatoes on this day, plus cabbage in some form. Try to drink as many as five glasses of water today to wash away the uric acid in your body. No more fruit today.
Sex snack	Carrot, cucumber, and celery sticks.

missionary position

On the grounds that your digestion feels more sluggish today thanks to the beef you are digesting, sex needs to be relaxed and easygoing. Missionary-position sex is ideal for this, plus it includes the benefit of being done face-to-face so that you can kiss and be as romantic as you like toward each other. See pp.48-53 for the missionary and its variations.

provoke or
be provoked!

The whole point of this exercise is to give your partner incredible sensual stimulation while doing your best to resist their own efforts on you. Most men and women like to have their erogenous zones played with during intercourse, since it makes the whole experience so much more erotic. So men, if you are taking your partner from the rear, reach around her with your hand and stimulate her clitoris. Women, if you are on top and moving as rapidly as you can manage, up his stimulation by grasping the base of his penis and letting your hand run up and down it, in rhythm with the in-out of your thrusting. The longer you can stop yourself from climaxing, the more thrusting you will manage and the greater the aerobic exercise. However...let's not forget that sex isn't really a competition, but more of a game. And some of the best experiences allow at least one of you to become a winner!

THE COMBINATION OF ALMOST two weeks' worth of careful eating, fresh foods, and some weight loss should mean that YOU, and not just your body, are feeling different. When we feel fitter we look at ourselves in the mirror with new eyes. We see someone who we suddenly perceive as being newly attractive, or energetic, or flexible. We may feel brisk enough to go dancing, or to practice acrobatics, or to walk to the yoga class instead of driving.

In fact, the more successful you feel you are, the better pleased you become with yourself and the more likely to want to celebrate sexually. Your instruction today, therefore, is to last as long as you possibly can during sex, even though your partner is doing everything in his/her power to make you climax. That should make for some fun!

eat me

Breakfast	Half a sweet grapefruit, but NO sugar.
Lunch	Grilled tomatoes and baked beans (the low-calorie variety).
Dinner	As on Day Six, dinner today consists of fish, preferably an oily one. This might be salmon or mackerel. Or if you prefer chewy white meat, consider plaice or sole. Microwave or grill the fish. Serve with cooked broccoli, a fresh green salad (that includes chopped white cabbage), and a few small new potatoes. Dessert consists of peeled halved or sliced peaches, sprinkled with a little brown sugar and browned under the grill. If you can't get fresh peaches, canned ones will do, so long as they are canned in juice, not syrup.
Sex snack	Fresh popcorn, without butter or sugar.

BY THE END OF THIS SECOND WEEK the 28-Day Plan should be sinking into your unconscious. The goal is to make the weekly routine of vegetables and fruit—and later in the week, meat—automatic. Part of the pattern is to think ahead, to keep in mind what shopping food preparation need to be done, even to the extent of knowing when you must cook in advance and when you can eat ad hoc. Of course, eating ad hoc depends on always stocking the right foods. It doesn't mean helping yourself to a candy bar!

Today is the last day when you have to cut out wheat and dairy products extirely (except for skimmed milk). So if you feel as though today's menu only partly satisfies you, hang in there. Next week may feel more satisfactory. Part of today's routine is to take a long walk in the open, preferably in a park or in the countryside, so that you thoroughly exercise the body while enjoying beautiful scenery. There are many ways of satisfying the senses, and getting different types of regular exercise during the Plan is extremely important.

loving touch

There isn't a position for today. This is the day of rest—the day when the two of you snuggle, hold each other closely, and talk intimately about the events of the day. Sex improves when you don't do it every day of the week—so this is your day off.

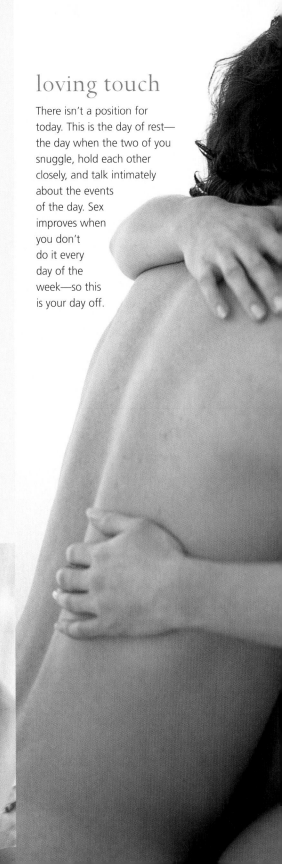

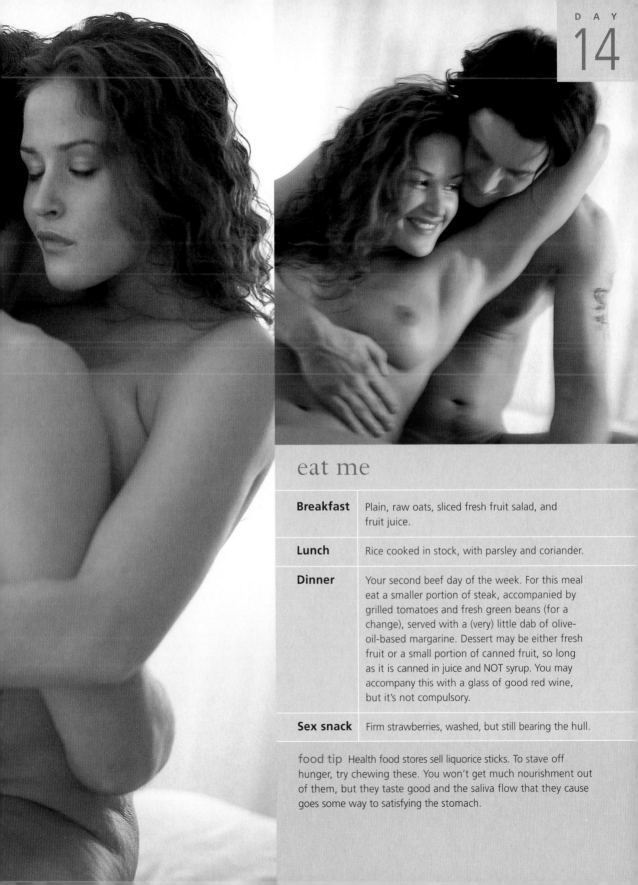

eat me

Breakfast	Plain, raw oats, sliced fresh fruit salad, and fruit juice.
Lunch	Rice cooked in stock, with parsley and coriander.
Dinner	Your second beef day of the week. For this meal eat a smaller portion of steak, accompanied by grilled tomatoes and fresh green beans (for a change), served with a (very) little dab of olive-oil-based margarine. Dessert may be either fresh fruit or a small portion of canned fruit, so long as it is canned in juice and NOT syrup. You may accompany this with a glass of good red wine, but it's not compulsory.
Sex snack	Firm strawberries, washed, but still bearing the hull.

food tip Health food stores sell liquorice sticks. To stave off hunger, try chewing these. You won't get much nourishment out of them, but they taste good and the saliva flow that they cause goes some way to satisfying the stomach.

"Watermelon—it's a good fruit. You eat, you drink, you wash your face."

Enrico Caruso

deeper penetration

In order to increase the flexibility of her thighs and of his buttocks and thighs, try one of the deep penetration positions. You might want to experiment with this version of the Missionary Position, where she lies on her back but with her legs back and her feet resting on his shoulders. She often feels pleasingly helpless in this pose, while he benefits from the novelty of the position. She should find her G-spot gets stimulated; remember that the G-spot responds best to steady pulsations of pressure rather than the friction of thrusting. If she doesn't experience too much sensation this way, lovemaking can easily be finished off with the more conventional missionary moves (see pp.48-53).

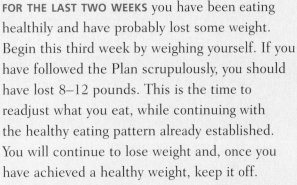

FOR THE LAST TWO WEEKS you have been eating healthily and have probably lost some weight. Begin this third week by weighing yourself. If you have followed the Plan scrupulously, you should have lost 8–12 pounds. This is the time to readjust what you eat, while continuing with the healthy eating pattern already established. You will continue to lose weight and, once you have achieved a healthy weight, keep it off.

During the last two weeks you have eliminated all wheat products from your diet and most dairy, with the exception of milk. Having detoxed your system of wheat, this week you will reintroduce it. Hopefully, you do not have a problem digesting wheat but if, like me, you find your stomach bloats almost immediately after eating it, this is useful, if unwelcome, news. You may adore bread but when you know it blows you up, you will look and feel a lot better by cutting it out of your diet for good.

eat me

Breakfast	A citrus fruit and a slice of toast. No butter or margarine on the toast, but a scraping of yeast extract spread very thinly is fine. Dry toast gets to taste fine. It's important to make it from really tasty bread like the seed bread described on p.149.
Lunch	Hearty vegetable soup (see p.146 for recipe). This can be made in advance and is especially good in winter when you want more than a salad. It can even be frozen. It is quick and easy to cook.
Dinner	Vegetable platter of plain cooked vegetables such as broccoli, cauliflower, zucchini, green beans.
Sex snack	A handful of seeds or a couple of sliced raw carrots. Resist filling up on bread.

IT'S ASSESSMENT DAY. How did your stomach and digestive system react to reintroducing wheat to your diet yesterday? How did you feel? Comfortable? Or in pain? Having done without wheat and wheat products for 14 days, your system will instantly react if it dislikes wheat and you reintroduce it now. If you find that your digestion tolerates the addition of bread with no difficulty, you can continue eating up to two slices a day, provided you do not want to lose more weight.

If your stomach hurts and feels bloated with gas, then try to do without the bread and other wheat products. You'll feel much sexier. There is something about possessing a flat stomach that makes you feel acrobatic and flexible, a slightly erotic sensation that bodes well for lovemaking. Today's menu continues the process of reintroducing foodstuffs (today it's egg) but if you want to lose more weight, substitute the menu given on Day Two (see p.93) for the one here.

the wheelbarrow

Occasionally it's fun to attempt something sexual that is probably impossible but that makes you laugh while trying. One of my favorite silly positions is the Wheelbarrow, where the woman balances on her hands and the man, who is standing, tucks her legs under his arm and enters her from the rear. This uses strength in her forearms and he needs to pivot well in order to be able to thrust properly (but not enough to actually knock his partner over!). The ability to try something silly is comforting because it means you trust your partner enough to risk looking foolish.

eat me

Breakfast	A lightly boiled egg and toast fingers with yeast extract (up to one slice of bread's worth). Or a bowl of cornflakes with skimmed milk, but no fruit.
Lunch	A large, raw, crunchy salad that includes white and red cabbage, thinly sliced carrot, sliced red pepper and cucumber, and shredded iceberg lettuce. Top with sunflower and sesame seeds, a very few linseeds (if you are female), and a tiny amount of low-calorie salad dressing. If you want bread, eat your second slice today here without any spread.
Supper	Chinese Stir Fry: this might include sliced mushrooms, water chestnuts, bamboo shoots, beansprouts, sliced carrots and green cabbage, spring onion, and a sprinkling of soy sauce (one without any sugar content) and Chinese seasoning for flavor. Wok all the ingredients in a little sesame seed oil. If you're no longer trying to lose weight, serve on a bed of rice noodles, otherwise leave these out. No fruit for dessert tonight.

sex tip If you have time to make love during the day, try drinking a cup of coffee half an hour beforehand. Coffee acts as a mild stimulant to the central nervous system. The stimulant effect peaks in the blood 15 to 45 minutes after you've drunk it. Try taking your coffee black, or if you find that unpalatable, use skimmed milk. But don't drink it after 6pm.

"There is no sincerer love than the love of food."

George Bernard Shaw

HOW DID YOUR STOMACH FEEL after eating yesterday's breakfast egg? As with wheat, you can deduce the effect of egg on your digestion when you reintroduce it, and if it feels uncomfortable and produces unacceptable levels of gas, leave it out in the future. But if it is fine, you can include a couple of eggs a week in your diet. For example, you could add slices of hard-boiled egg to today's green and white salad.

Day Three is a day that, with the exception of breakfast, tries to do without any substance containing sugar. In practice, this means no further fruit. But it is not a good idea to cut out fruit from the breakfast meal, since the juicy fiber in fruit helps your digestive system function efficiently.

time on your own

Take turns having a warm bath and a self massage. After the bath, cover your body with a quality moisturizing lotion. There are some popular brands that contain almond oil that are ideal. They spread on the body easily, they don't stain, nor do they clog the pores so much that you feel you need a second bath. Provided they are massaged in firmly, they also feel slightly warmer to the body than other lotions. All massages feel better when the sensation is warm rather than cold and a self-massage is no exception. So move from your warm bath to a warm bedroom and spend 20 minutes on slowly and enjoyably massaging yourself with small circular strokes. If you feel like it, include the genitals at the end of the massage—this is optional.

eat me

Breakfast	Two tangerines, or half a melon, or half a large pink grapefruit. After a couple of weeks managing without sugar, you find that the natural sweetness in food substances is easier to detect.
Lunch	Green and white salad of chopped crisp lettuce. I use Bibb, romaine, and iceberg with fresh watercress (well washed), a few green olives, torn-up strands of herbs such as basil, parsley, and cilantro. Add white cannelini beans to the middle and, if you're no longer trying to lose weight, small squares of feta cheese. Eat as much as you can.
Supper	Colcannon is an Irish dish that has traditionally been favored for fast-day celebrations when meat would not be eaten. This can be prepared in advance and frozen (see p.147 for recipe).
Sex snack	If you are wheat tolerant, try toast fingers spread with yeast extract.

ONE OF THE GREAT SIDE-EFFECTS of good eating, gradual weight loss, and better health is that your stamina improves. If you have managed to do without tobacco and alcohol during the Plan so far, so much the better for your lungs, blood oxygenization, and arterial health. Men and women with a healthy blood supply find that sexual arousal happens easily.

Aiming for marathon sex is generally not a good idea. It's not how long you have sex that is arousing, but the imagination and technique you bring to loving. If, however, you are already full of imagination and have great technique, it still helps not to be covered in perspiration or to get tired out after only three minutes of intercourse. Taking your time over sex is to be recommended.

eat me

Breakfast	Bananas and cornflakes and skimmed milk—as much as you like.
Lunch	The usual varied salad, complete with seeds and shredded cabbage, and a small amount of salad dressing. Dessert can be bananas and milk. One slice of bread if you are eating it.
Dinner	Easy-stuffed cabbage (see p.147 for recipe). Easy because, although you make the stuffing, you don't have to fill the center of the cabbage. It may not look as picturesque as real stuffed cabbage but if you lay the cooked stuffing beside the cooked cabbage the taste is much the same! Dessert consists of sliced bananas, sliced apple, and halved green grapes with seeds left in. (The seeds contain a substance that is sudden death to candida.)
Sex snack	Melon—tons of it. And leave it out of the refrigerator so that it ripens and becomes sweet.

an old-fashioned girl

The Lyons Stagecoach is a sex position that featured in 17th-, 18th-, and 19th-century sex books and presumably gained its name from emulating the kind of bumpy ride you received should you ever have traveled anywhere in an old-fashioned stagecoach. It's a woman-on-top position that requires strong arms (these hold the weight of your body) and a strong back.

Both partners sit up and face each other. She sits astride his penis with her legs on each side of his hips and leans back on her hands. He also leans back on his hands. This way both partners remain (more or less) upright while she levers herself up and down during her bumpy coach ride. It takes stamina to keep going!

THIS IS ONE OF THOSE evenings when it's a good idea to take a romantic walk. A gentle stroll in the night air is healthily relaxing. It offers enough exercise to make you feel at ease, but it's not so strenuous that you want to fall asleep right afterward. It's just right, in fact, for the kind of sex that takes pressure off the abdomen yet gives a gentle satisfaction to round off the day.

One of the problems with eating meat dishes, such as the beef that you'll be eating today, is that they take quite a long time to digest. If you eat later in the evening, you may find that your delicious steak is still sitting in your stomach when you go to bed. A gentle walk will give your body time to digest your food and leave you in just the right mood for great sex.

eat me

Breakfast	A whole ripe papaya cut in half and eaten with the seeds (for roughage).
Lunch	Halved tomatoes, brushed with olive oil and sprinkled with salt, pepper, basil, and rosemary. Grill them, and serve on a slice of seed-bread toast.
Dinner	Lean, ground beef, cooked in a nonstick frying pan with a small amount of olive oil, a dash of garlic, Worcestershire sauce, and seasoning. Before serving, drain off all cooking fat. Serve with a tomato sauce made of chopped skinned tomatoes that have been liquidized, then gently heated with a tiny amount of seasoning, plus broccoli and sliced green beans. The easiest method to skin tomatoes is to plunge them in boiling water for a short time. Try to drink as many as five glasses of water today to wash away the uric acid in your body. No more fruit today.
Sex snack	Celery, carrot sticks, and water.

"Ice cream is exquisite. What a pity it isn't illegal."

Voltaire

sex from the rear

While she kneels on the floor with the upper half of her body leaning across the bed, he kneels behind her and thrusts from the rear. One of his hands can reach around her hips so that he is in a position to stroke her clitoris while penetrating her vagina. This is an extremely comfortable position for him, although he needs to use a lot of buttock movement. It's comfortable for her too, provided she doesn't rest her abdomen or upper half against the bed.

INSTEAD OF DRINKING red wine, tonight you are cooking with it. Tonight also sees chicken come on to the menu. Chicken can cause an allergic reaction in some people, so once again, assess how your digestion reacts to this meat after the meal. Since you are trying to keep your diet as free of animal fat as possible, cut every fraction of fat from the chicken pieces.

As an additional celebration to the red wine, you can enjoy a cool fruit sorbet ice—even if it does contain some sugar! One of the problems of careful eating is the monotony of the food allowed since so much is "forbidden." Transfer your yearnings for food into great sex with your lover. Don't eat too much at your evening meal. Remember, a light stomach makes an energetic lover!

> **"**An apple is an excellent thing... until you have tried a peach.**"**
>
> George du Maurier

eat me

Breakfast	Fresh fruit or a dollop of stewed apples or pears cooked in fruit juice but without additional sugar.
Lunch	Spinach, broccoli, and green bean bake (see p.148 for recipe). You can eat this dish hot or cold, depending on the season. The bake can be prepared in advance, left to cool, and then kept in the refrigerator until needed. In all, preparation takes about an hour.
Dinner	Jeremy's Chinese chicken casserole. This consists of chicken and cabbage cooked together in red wine (see p.148 for the full recipe). Serve the casserole with plain rice. The casserole can be prepared in advance and kept in a fridge or freezer. Dessert is a plain fruit sorbet, bought, not made. Check the labels and select one with no milk or cream.
Sex snack	Rice crackers spread with a little yeast extract.

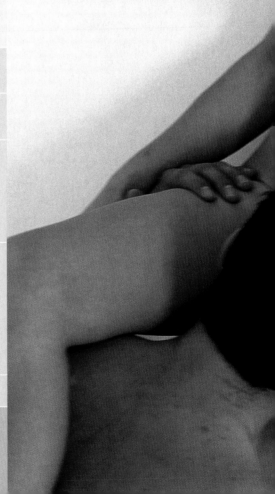

The oral banquet

This is where you find out if your practice with tongue exercises (see p.17) has paid off. Tonight you are going to give her the best oral sex she has ever enjoyed. Tomorrow it is her turn to pleasure you.

For really sensational cunnilingus, your head needs to be right between her thighs and preferably slightly below them so that you can stroke upward with your tongue against the shaft of her clitoris.

From here you can also occasionally insert the tip of your tongue into her vagina.

But it's the clitoris that experiences most sensation. Experiment with the tip of the tongue in featherlight twirling on top of the clitoris itself.

Try stimulating one side of the clitoris and then the other, but always from underneath. Often one side of the clitoris seems more sensitive than the other.

Ask her for feedback so that you can learn what she likes best.

AT THE END OF THIS THIRD WEEK you will
have just undergone an elimination diet.
Having eliminated food substances
known to be allergens, we have slowly
brought them back into your diet to
find out how they affect you. Hopefully,
you will suffer little or no discomfort
from doing so.

The menu for the last week is a kind
of "holding menu," which establishes
a healthy food routine that will prevent
more weight gain. If you want to lose
more weight, the best way to do so is
to return to the first week of the 28-Day
Plan, repeating it until you have gained
your desired size and shape. Use the Plan as
a basis for your diet for the rest of your life.
It keeps you fit and trim and in wonderful
shape for a healthy sex life.

eat me

Breakfast	Plain, raw oats, sliced, fresh fruit salad, and fruit juice.
Lunch	Salade Niçoise. Dress with a plain olive oil and balsamic vinegar dressing. Accompany by one slice of seed bread (see pp.148-49 for recipes).
Dinner	If you are no longer trying to lose weight, have grilled mackerel or salmon, accompanied by an assortment of vegetables, excluding peas and corn. If you are still trying to lose weight, leave out the fish and eat more veg. Dessert can be a mixture of soft fruits.
Sex snack	You are allowed 3½ oz (100g) of dark chocolate, but no more. Share the remainder with friends.

oral sex for him

There are a number of ways in which you can provoke exquisite sensation in your man's penis. Try licking the penis as if it were a delicious ice-cream cone. Hold the base of the penis in one hand and then, using the blade of your tongue, lick up from the base of the penis, first on one side and then the other. Next, take the penis between your lips and slide your mouth gradually down to the base and back. Be careful to avoid nipping him with your teeth. Try sucking on the head of the penis and then letting go, then sucking again. You can also experiment with the butterfly flick. This involves flicking your tongue lightly across and along the ridge on the underside of the penis.

131

IN THE FINAL WEEK OF THE PLAN you firmly establish your personal healthy eating pattern. This may include eating more bread, so that you don't feel hungry, or occasional eggs, to give variety to your diet. But the overall pattern of high fiber, low fat, low sugar, little carbohydrate, and occasional protein is what counts. Continue to use the seven-day unit of the 28-Day Plan where the first four days of the diet consist of vegetables only.

Similarly, the sexual side of the plan is totally noncompulsory. I suggest tailoring your sexual activity to follow how your digestion is behaving and also what day of the week it is. No one should ever have sex when they don't want to, so use my ideas as suggestions only and adapt accordingly!

the yawning position

The *Kama Sutra* mentions this position where the woman lies on her back with her legs on both sides of her partner's hips, held as wide open as she can comfortably manage. He thrusts from a kneeling position. The woman's thigh stretch exercises all her inner thigh muscles and leaves her feeling open and vulnerable, something that many women find extremely erotic. Any woman who has done her Pilates thigh stretch (see p.31) will get a great deal out of this one.

eat me

Breakfast	One large piece of fruit such as orange, sweet grapefruit, or half a melon.
Lunch	Three bean salad (see p.149 for recipe). Old-fashioned cooks were religious about cooking their own beans, spending hours on it. These days, life is just too short, and since canned beans are now excellently prepared and readily available, I use these. Garnish with chopped parsley and a lemon wedge. For variety, mix fresh green beans with canned beans. Accompany with a slice of bread.
Dinner	Eat as much of the cabbage casserole as you want (see p.146 for recipe). If you are eating bread, use up one of your slices here. If not, prepare either plain boiled potatoes or a baked potato. Cover the potatoes with the vegetable mixture so that the fluffy potato is soaked through and you won't feel the need for extra butter or margarine. For dessert, you can finish the other half of the melon.
Sex snack	As much raw celery as you can eat. Or the other half of the melon, if you haven't had it for dinner.

THE FIRST PROVISO OF SEX is that it should be enjoyable. The second is that it should be something you want to do. And if you're following the 28-Day Plan, the third is that it offers you a physical as well as a sensual workout—however mild. If you've persevered with the exercises in Chapter Two you'll know that some of them are Pilates training moves.

When you come to today's sex position you will see that it's a pleasurable version of a basic Pilates thigh stretch (a little like the move on p.31). Your lover just happens to be between your thighs while you are training. And as you stretch wide you will also get a sense of how your eating plan is affecting you. If your stomach now feels comfortable and your food digestion easy, you'll enjoy the sexual side of the 28-Day Plan a lot more.

> "I often take exercise. Why, only yesterday I had my breakfast in bed."
>
> Oscar Wilde

eat me

Breakfast	A big piece of fruit such as a large apple or a small bunch of grapes.
Lunch	A fresh salad of chopped white cabbage, sweet orange, Belgian endive, and sunflower seeds with a garlic-flavored dressing. Eat with a slice of bread.
Dinner	Wok-fried white cabbage with onion, mushroom, sliced potato, and grated apple. Season with a light curry powder and a little water. Cover to cook. Shortly before serving stir in finely chopped cilantro. Serve on a bed of heated canned lentils that have been flavored with cumin and coriander.
Sex snack	Prepare a box of fresh carrot, celery, red pepper, and raw cauliflower cut into sticks or florets.

drinks Drink only tea, black coffee or water today—do not drink any fruit juices.

pillow talk

Here the woman lies on her back with her buttocks propped up on
a pillow. The man thrusts between her legs and encourages her to lift her buttocks up
in order to get closer to him, meeting him halfway. Her clitoris meets his genitals with greater
impact and she uses the core stability of her abdomen, together with very strong buttock
motion. She might also like to exercise her vaginal muscles on her man at the same time.

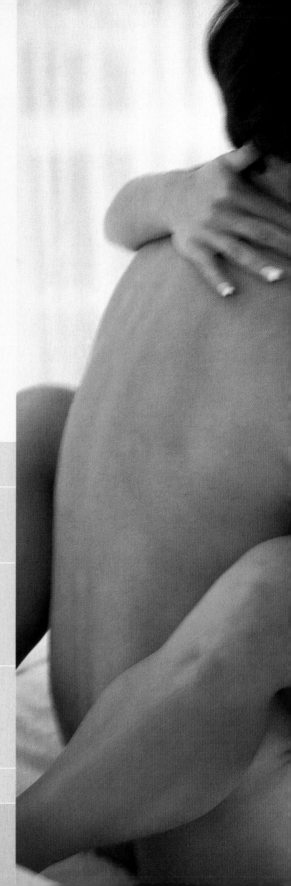

ANYONE WHO HAS EVER TAKEN UP horseback riding will understand the similarities between riding rhythms and certain sex positions. Despite the coarse jokes, it's no coincidence that teenage girls often adore horses and horsy activities. Sensuality increases during puberty and it's perfectly common for young women to experience their first orgasm in the saddle. No wonder they become hooked.

But if you've never had the opportunity to discover your sexual response through horsemanship, fear not. Today's sex position exercises exactly those muscles used when pounding through the fields at a trot. If you persevere, you might even be able to train yourself to ride a real horse, should the inclination sweep you into the stables!

eat me

Breakfast	One large portion of fruit—a peach, half a melon, or a large apple. If you are still having difficulties with digestion, include three or four canned prunes—canned in fruit juice, NOT syrup.
Lunch	A large salad on a bed of lentils, chopped apple with red peel left on the outside, baby plum tomatoes cut in halves, and baby spinach leaves. Season with salt and pepper and a plain olive oil and balsamic vinegar dressing. Eat with a slice of bread. Dessert is a large apple.
Dinner	Red cabbage with grated apple, a drop of balsamic vinegar, sultanas, and sunflower seeds wok-fried in olive oil. If you're no longer going for weight loss serve with a baked potato. If you are, replace the potato with two green vegetables. Dessert is soft fruit, such as raspberries or strawberries.
Sex snack	A second slice of bread or wheat-free rice crackers.

"The perfect lover is one who turns into pizza at 4 am."

Charles Pierce

pounding on the spot

The 16th-century sex manual *The Perfumed Garden* describes a sex position called Pounding on the Spot. The man sits with his legs outstretched and the woman sits astride and facing him with her legs wrapped around his waist, guiding his penis into her vagina. The position feels similar to horseback riding, because the movement of her thigh muscles in rising and falling on her man is very similar to rising to the trot when on horseback. The man's pleasure can be greatly enhanced if every time she slides down his penis she also tightens her vaginal muscles to grasp him firmly. Both buttock and vaginal muscles come into play here.

IT'S OFTEN ONLY AFTER YOU'VE finished making love that you realize just how long you have been able to continue a particularly energetic activity. It's interesting to observe which muscles you use during certain sex sessions. Today's sex position relies on a lot of stamina and extrastrong thigh and buttock muscles in the man. These allow upward and downward thrusting to continue for a long time. I'm not suggesting that sexual intercourse become a stamina test, but I do know that many women need their man to last a long time, so that they (the women) can climax. However, if prolonged intercourse doesn't work for you, take a look at tomorrow's sex position instead.

man underneath

Although the woman is on top, it is the man underneath who makes this work and is in control of this lovemaking session. He lies with his legs apart so that she can lie on top of him face-to-face, her legs between his, supporting her weight on her forearms. She may, of course, move but the main action comes from his thrusting upward, a mixture of thigh and buttock action. When you get tired, roll over while still embracing and go for thrusting in the Missionary Position.

eat me

Breakfast	Bananas and skimmed milk—as much as you can eat and drink.
Lunch	A large, mixed salad, complete with seeds and shredded cabbage and a small amount of salad dressing. Dessert can be bananas and milk.
Dinner	Baked ratatouille (see p.149 for recipe).
Sex snack	Those curvy yellow fruits again.

drinks Skimmed milk, tea, coffee—provided it is drunk no later than 6 pm—and water.

MANY WOMEN DON'T WANT their man to continue pounding for hours during sex. It may be athletic, but it is also boring. Instead they would far prefer some magic fingerwork. What turns women on is kissing, caressing, bodies touching as close together as possible, and a long, long time spent on romantic buildup. Ideally, caressing starts on the upper half of the body and works its way around to the pelvic area. Nor is it done in a kind of vacuum.

Imagination makes any sex work well and this can be fueled by words of love, naughty suggestions, or even by erotic stories while his magic fingers carry out their mission. Just keep in mind that good sex is about being loving as well as being physical. Tell your woman how much you love her while you give her magic moments with your hands.

eat me

Breakfast	Purée in the blender exotic fruits such as mango, papaya, strawberries, anything except banana.
Lunch	Vegetable soup (for recipe see p.146). This can be prepared in advance and put into a thermos to take to work. Dessert is a ripe papaya or mango. If you eat papaya, swallow down the seeds and pulp from the middle—it's fantastically good for you.
Supper	Tonight is steak night again. Eat up to 20oz of grilled beef, accompanied by grilled tomatoes and one green vegetable. Dessert may be either fresh fruit or a small portion of canned fruit, provided it is canned in juice and NOT syrup.
Sex snack	Rice crackers thinly spread with yeast extract.

tip Drink at least five glasses of water during the day to flush away the uric acid.

magic fingerwork

Only after you have stroked your lover's entire body with your fingertips should you progress to stroking her genitals. Make sure her genitals are well lubricated—there are special oils designed for this or, if you can't afford them, try good, old-fashioned saliva. Once you've reached her genitals here are four great massage moves.

Gentle hair torture Pull her pubic hair gently and in small tufts. Using both hands at a time, work your way from the top of her pubic hair down each side of the labia.

Duck's bill Shape the fingers of one hand into a "duck's bill," hold them above her clitoris and pour warmed massage oil over them so that it slowly seeps through and onto her genitals.

Wibbling Pull one of her vaginal lips and let go. Then repeat a little farther down the lips. Work your way down one labia and then repeat the "wibbling" on the other.

Clitoral maneuvers With featherlight touch and plenty of lubrication run your finger first around the head and then up and down the shaft of the clitoris.

"There are four basic food groups: milk chocolate, dark chocolate, white chocolate, and chocolate truffles."

ONE OF MEN'S COMPLAINTS about women is that they don't take the initiative often enough during lovemaking. Another grumble is that, after some years, sex, however enjoyably it works, gets boring. This is why it's a good idea occasionally to throw in something new and dynamic. Don't do it too often, though, because it's important to keep a surprise factor. We are novelty-seeking creatures and the bedroom is no exception to this.

Today, therefore, the woman is going to offer her man the wonderful manual treat that yesterday he was generous enough to practice on her. Only this is a version especially tailored to the male anatomy. You might also like to try the experiment of performing it before the evening meal—that is, if you are single, childfree, and workfree. Otherwise, eat lightly tonight!

eat me

Breakfast	A half or even a whole sweet grapefruit, but with no additional sugar.
Lunch	A huge crunchy salad if it's summer or a homemade vegetable soup if its winter. A slice of seed bread.
Dinner	A meaty, textured white fish such as sole, brill, or turbot, cooked with seeded grape halves in a little olive oil. You might also like to try the experiment of cooking it with samphire, an edible seaweed. Even if you don't like the texture of samphire (it needs to be tender), it adds a naturally saltiness to the food. Serve the fish of your choice with a selection of green vegetables. Dessert is Phillip's Egg Custard (for recipe see p.149)
Sex snack	Chopped fresh vegetables such as carrots, celery, cauliflower florets, red or green pepper.

genital massage

Cover your man's body with caresses and work your way down to his genitals. You're going to give him a genital massage. Ensure that your hands are well oiled so that your skin doesn't catch on the delicate skin of his penis. Here are three strokes to bring him pleasure:

The Lemon Squeezer Steady the penis around the shaft with one hand and rub the cupped palm of the other over and around the head of the penis as if you were juicing a lemon.

Hand over Hand Slide your cupped hand over the head and down the shaft. Before it gets down to the base, bring the other hand up to start the process again at the top so that the downward movement is like a continuous stream.

The Countdown This consists of two strokes. For the first, grasp the top of his penis with your right hand and place your left hand underneath his testicles, with fingers positioned toward the anus. As you slide your right hand down the penis shaft, enclosing it as much as possible, bring your left hand up from his testicles. Aim to bring both hands slowly together at the base of the shaft. For the second, slide your right hand back up his penis from the base while simultaneously bringing your left hand back under his testicles again. As before, work slowly and steadily. Your count now goes:
10 times the first stroke, then 10 times the second;
Nine times the first stroke, then nine times the second;
And so on, right on down to one stroke.

DURING THE PAST MONTH you should have lost some weight (if that was your goal); learned to eat healthy food; learned healthy patterns of eating so that you can easily, even automatically, continue the Plan on a weekly basis; detoxed your body of harmful food substances; learned to listen to what your stomach is telling you about your individual digestive capability; and gained greater flexibility of the body as a result. If you dislike any part of this food plan,

you can tailor it to suit you personally—just so long as you stick to the weekly pattern of eating and cut out most fats. Along the way I also hope you learned to tailor your lovemaking, not just to each other's emotional needs but also to those of your body, and—crazy though it sounds—to your stomach. You don't really need me to tell you that if you are suffering from indigestion or you are seriously overweight you aren't going to feel a lot like making love.

eat me

Breakfast	Fresh fruit salad.
Lunch	Freshly cooked new potatoes, tossed with olive-oil-based margarine and chopped basil, with a plate of shredded cabbage, carrot, and apple, tossed in lemon juice. Eat with a slice of bread
Dinner	Beef and tomatoes (see p.99), serve with green vegetables and a slice of bread. Dessert may be either fresh fruit or a small portion of canned fruit, provided it is canned in juice and not syrup.
Sex snack	Melon—tons of it. And leave it out of the refrigerator so that it ripens and becomes sweet.

food tip Drink at least five glasses of water today to wash the uric acid from the body.

side-by-side clasping

If you feel like showing off you might go for the crazy acrobatic feat described on p.23 called the Bridge Pose. But if you feel a little too full of beef something slower and easier might fit the bill. Side-by-side lovemaking works well for men and women wanting to take their sex lives at a slightly slower pace so here, as an option, is the Side-by-Side Clasping Position. Lie on your sides facing each other with your legs outstretched. Her upper leg is between his legs and his penis is in her vagina. He places a hand on her buttocks and gently pulls her toward him. She then lets go so that he is using her whole body to facilitate intercourse. If you prefer a more energetic version of clasping, roll over so that the woman is on her back and her lover is stretched along her body with his legs wrapped around hers.

recipes

THE FOLLOWING RECIPES ARE REFERRED to in the 28-Day Plan. When adapting them to your own requirements, check the guidelines on p.82 to ensure that you stick to the spirit of the Plan.

---

vegetable soup
day 1

Ingredients

2 medium-sized potatoes
2 large carrots
¼lb green cabbage
half a leek
1 vegetable stock cube

Method

Drop the potatoes, carrots, cabbage, and leek into two pints of water. You don't have to chop or slice any of the vegetables. In fact, there's only one proviso before cooking, which is that the vegetables need to be scrubbed clean first. You can also add vegetable leftovers if you like being thrifty. Add one vegetable stock cube. Simmer for half an hour or until the carrots are cooked through. When cool, blend in the mixer. Don't add salt and pepper until you have finished blending. The cutting action of the blender blades strengthens the salt and pepper flavor and often overseasons. You can adjust the thickness of the soup by adding or reducing the soup liquid.

---

cabbage casserole
day 3

Ingredients

2 large field mushrooms, sliced
3 large carrots, chopped
1 large leek, chopped
a generous portion of thin
   green beans, trimmed and
   cut in half
½lb white cabbage, chopped
2 stalks of celery, chopped (optional)

Method

Simmer all these ingredients in enough vegetable or beef stock to cover. Add a small amount of salt to taste. Cook slowly until all ingredients are tender but not slushy. This will probably take around 20 minutes, but test from time to time. You can, if you like, make this in a much larger quantity and keep the extra in the refrigerator. You can also store it in a thermos, so it's convenient to transport.

cabbage moussaka
day 11

Ingredients

1 small white cabbage, chopped
1 leek, chopped
3 large carrots, thinly sliced
2 tbs olive oil
garlic granules
½lb potatoes, peeled and cut into slices

Method

Lightly heat the shredded white cabbage, chopped leek, and thinly sliced carrots in a little olive oil with the garlic granules. When this is coated with oil and beginning to soften, transfer half the mixture into an ovenproof casserole dish. Cover with the sliced potato pieces, season with salt, pepper, and freshly grated nutmeg. Transfer the reserved portion of softened vegetables and spread evenly, then top with further sliced potato pieces. Season again with salt, pepper, and freshly grated nutmeg. Make up a sauce of skimmed milk and ground rice, so that the sauce thickens slightly but is fluid. Pour onto the casserole until the layers are covered and then dot the top with dabs of olive-oil-based margarine. Bake at 300 degrees for 30 minutes.

colcannon
day 17

This is an Irish dish favored on fast-day celebrations when meat was not eaten. The dish can be prepared in advance and then frozen.

Ingredients

1 small bowl of mashed potato
1 small bowl of lightly cooked, chopped cabbage, preferably the green variety
1 large onion, chopped
1 tbs olive oil

Method

Mix the mashed potato and cabbage together thoroughly in a large mixing bowl. Cook the chopped onion with the olive oil in a wok, then add the potato and cabbage mixture, pressing the mixture down firmly into the softened onion. The mixture should flatten out and cook to an even brown underneath. When the mixture has cooked to the point of crusting, turn it over and cook the other side. Press the mixture into the wok from time to time and continue cooking and turning until you end up with a green and white marbled cake with tasty, crispy brown bits.

easy-stuffed cabbage
day 18

Ingredients

1lb cooked, long-grain rice
1 tbs olive oil
garlic granules
1 small onion, sliced
½lb mushrooms, sliced and lightly cooked
2 tomatoes, skinned and chopped
a handful of sultanas
1 vegetable stock cube
pepper, salt, Worcestershire sauce

Method

The stuffing consists of ready-cooked, long-grain rice cooked in olive oil with the garlic granules, sliced onion, and mushrooms. (This can be prepared in advance and frozen in suitable quantities.) Add to the mixture two skinned, chopped tomatoes, and a handful of sultanas and flavor with a vegetable stock cube, pepper, salt, and Worcestershire sauce. When the rice mixture is fully cooked, serve it with plain-boiled, green cabbage.

spinach, broccoli, and green bean bake
day 20

This dish can be prepared in advance and kept in the fridge until needed.

Ingredients
1lb spinach
1lb broccoli, broken into florets
a handful of thin green beans
2 eggs
½ pint of skimmed milk
salt and pepper

Method
Thoroughly clean the spinach, take off any coarse stalks, and blanch. Blanch the broccoli florets. Chop the thin, green beans into 2-inch portions and blanch. All three vegetables can be precooked together. Arrange these in an ovenproof dish and season with salt and pepper. Whisk two eggs into half a pint of skimmed milk and pour the frothing mixture over the vegetables. Grate fresh nutmeg on the top. Bake in the oven at 350 degrees for 30-40 minutes. After about half an hour, test by putting a skewer into the mixture. If the skewer comes out clean, it's ready.

jeremy's chinese chicken casserole
day 20

Ingredients
the heart of a large white cabbage, chopped
1 tsp sesame oil
1 piece fresh, chopped root ginger
2 cloves garlic, chopped
1 chicken breast per person
½ pint vegetable stock
3 tbs red wine
1 dried chili pepper (optional)

Method
Cut the hard middle out of a white cabbage, chop it up, and then fry it in a little sesame oil with the fresh, chopped ginger and garlic. The taste of the core is altered and the texture is softened up. Pour the mixture into a casserole dish. Cut the rest of the cabbage up and add to the casserole. (A whole, large cabbage feeds four people.) Cut the chicken up and add to the casserole. You can use any part of the chicken but it needs to be taken off the bone. White breast meat tends to look the best but is not necessarily as tasty. Figure on a chicken breast per person. Add the vegetable stock and the red wine. If you like your meals really spicy, you can crumble the chilli pepper on top. Cook the casserole in a hot oven for one hour. Take it out, adjust the seasoning, and add extra wine if desired. Then return to the oven until the chicken is so tender it is almost in shreds. Serve with plain rice.

salade niçoise
day 21

Ingredients
1 romaine lettuce
4 oz canned or fresh, flaked tuna
a handful of black, pitted olives
2 hard-boiled egg halves per person
a few canned anchovies, chopped
olive oil and balsamic vinegar dressing

Method
Arrange the crisp romaine lettuce leaves like spears around the sides of the salad bowl and then put some chopped leaves at the bottom of the bowl as a bed. Place the flaked tuna in the middle. If you are using the canned variety, select tuna that is preserved in water or brine, not oil. Arrange the black, pitted olives, hard-boiled egg halves, and a few chopped, canned anchovies on top of the lettuce and tuna. Dress with a plain olive oil and balsamic vinegar dressing. Accompany with one slice of seed bread.

three-bean salad
day 22

Ingredients
1 can of chick peas
1 can of red kidney beans
1 can of cannellini beans
a handful of cooked, thin green beans
2 tbs finely chopped spring onions
1 tbs fresh parsley, tender mint, and
  cilantro
salt and pepper
garlic-flavored dressing

Method
Mix together the cans of chick peas, red kidney beans, and cannellini beans and wash thoroughly in a colander. Cut the green beans into 2-inch pieces and stir them into the bean mixture (green bean leftovers can be used up here) along with the finely chopped spring onions, fresh parsley, tender mint, and cilantro. Add a little salt and pepper and dress with a garlic-flavored dressing. Accompany with one slice of bread.

baked ratatouille
day 25

Ingredients
2 zucchinis, sliced
1lb tomatoes, skinned and sliced
1 tin cannellini beans
garlic salt
1 vegetable stock cube
salt and pepper
shredded green cabbage (optional)
tomato purée (optional)

Method
In a lightly oiled casserole dish, place the zucchinis, tomatoes, and cannellini beans in layers. Season each layer with garlic salt, crumbled vegetable stock cube, and season with salt and pepper. Dot the surface with small dabs of olive-oil-based margarine. If you want to continue using cabbage, you can also add shredded green cabbage to the layers. Bake at 350 degrees for half an hour, then test. For a stronger taste add tomato purée, but be aware that this virtually always contains sugar.

sexual seed bread

This recipe is written for those who use bread-baking machines to turn out their daily bread. It can, of course, be adapted to breadmaking by hand. The sexual aspect lies in the seeds, which benefit your sexual health, especially if you are female.

Ingredients
1 cup of tepid water
2½ tbs good-quality olive oil
1 tsp sugar
1 tsp salt
1 packet of yeast
1lb of flour (half white flour, half
  wholewheat)
seeds of your choice

Method
Reserve a little of the flour. Tip the rest of the ingredients into the container, with the flour against one side of the container so that it piles up against it. Put the container back in the machine gently, turn to ensure it's in the correct, locked position. With a spoon, make an indent in the dry part of the flour. Pour the packet of yeast into the indent. On no account must the yeast come into contact with the liquid at this stage, as it will start working immediately. Gently pour the remainder of the flour on top of this mixture. Switch on and once the machine starts mixing, reopen the lid and pour in any extra seeds. You might want to add sesame seeds, poppy seeds, pumpkin seeds, sunflower seeds. Linseeds are high in omega oils but don't taste terribly pleasant, so only include a few. You don't want the taste of them to dominate the loaf. Pine kernels and finely chopped mixed nuts are also possibilities. You may need to free up the edges of the dough with a spatula. If it begins to look too dry, add a little more water. Close the machine and come back to it three hours later. Take the loaf out as soon as possible.

index

acknowledgments

DK would like to thank photographer Russell Sadur and his
assistant, Nina Duncan; Toko for hair and make-up; Lynne
O'Neill, Carla DeAbreu, Maria Annison and Cheryl Stannard
for assisting on photoshoots; Laurence Errington for the index.
All photographs © Dorling Kindersley.